The Promotion of Culturally Responsive Teaching for Student Inclusion and Equality

Teaching Methods for the Education of Children from Diverse, Multicultural Backgrounds Paired With Parent Collaboration

Debera Perry

Table of Contents

Introduction

As every parent knows, a good education is key to raising capable children who become successful adults. Providing our children with the resources they need to thrive is an integral part of education. Some kids, however, struggle in school, regardless of what opportunities and resources are provided to them. Seeing their kids struggle is a source of worry for many parents and guardians, as well as educators. It is also a source of frustration. Parents often grow frustrated with their children when they fall behind in class because—having provided them with the best education available—they cannot quite see why they struggle. Educators similarly grow frustrated because they feel that their efforts to teach their students become stymied, and they want their students to learn. Getting frustrated, however, seldom helps parents, guardians, or educators. On the contrary, it proves detrimental to whatever they are trying to achieve. It prevents them from identifying the prevalent problem in the education system preventing children from learning. This core problem is that education is often treated as a uniform methodology.

There is a "one size fits all" mentality that is seen in numerous schools and institutions. This methodology fails to take the individual needs of students. It fails to account for their unique abilities, strengths, and weaknesses. Why? Because it fails to recognize that students are individual human beings with their own beliefs, values, interests, thoughts, learning methods, feelings, and more. True, for some students, the traditional learning methodologies work. Students whose learning methods and needs fit the structure of the pre-existing education system thrive in school. Students whose learning methods do not match the pre-existing education system, on the other hand, do not. A student who is very good at memorizing facts, for instance, will likely do well at school. How could he not? Seeing as the education system is primarily built on rote memorization.

Unlike the first student, another student who is not good at memorization but is good at learning by doing does not do as well at school. This is because the methodology that this student needs to be able to learn needs to be taken into account by the education system. This, however, isn't what student number two sees. What they see and perceive is that they have failed. Their difficulty memorizing things, no matter how hard they study, becomes a learning barrier. The more they encounter this barrier, the more they become disheartened by it. Over time, the situation demoralizes the student more and more, making them avoid studying. The student maybe even becomes prone to skipping class. Their grades suffer even more because of this situation, and the student soon finds themselves trapped in a seemingly unbreakable loop. Convinced that they're not cut out for school and can never get things right, they start considering dropping out, thus putting their future life, success, and livelihood at risk.

The scenario above exemplifies an endemic problem within traditional teaching methods. Put simply, the education system as it exists today does not consider students' different needs. It thus fails to give them equal opportunities to learn and be successful. I should know. I grew up in the public education system and witnessed this failure many times. At times, I struggled academically because of my own diverse background. Had a methodology that accounted for my individual needs been in place, however, students like me and I would have been able to thrive like some of our other classmates. This is why the methodology known as culturally responsive teaching is so important. Culturally responsive teaching is a research-based kind of teaching. It links students' experiences, languages, and even cultures to the subjects they learn in school. In doing so, it makes those subject matters more relatable, understandable, and personal. It also considers every student's unique learning needs and tailors teaching methodologies according to them.

It is only in recent years that culturally responsive teaching has become a fully recognized methodology. Still, it is not a very well-known one. Most schools and institutions have yet to adopt culturally responsive teaching, much to my disappointment. The fact that the education system largely has not adopted this methodology means that, for the most part, it does not give students from diverse backgrounds equal opportunity. As a result, some students—like me— struggle in school because of their diverse backgrounds. Others struggled because they experienced socioeconomic difficulties. They might not, for instance, possess the resources they need, such as a stable internet connection, computers, or even parental support and guidance to perform well and on equal fitting with their peers. Still, others might be facing language barriers. That means that a student might not be able to speak English at all or at the same level as their classmates. Alternatively, their parents and guardians might not be able to speak English or speak English well, making it challenging for them to communicate with teachers and educators and thus keep track of their children's academic progress.

In writing this book, I aim to awaken educators, parents, and guardians to the importance of diversity in every sense of the word. It is to enable educators, parents, and guardians to work together so that today's students can develop the skills they will need as independent adults, able to support themselves without having to depend on minimum-wage jobs.

When I was a student, I sometimes needed help with my studies. Yet, my parents were able to step up for my educational needs to provide the academic support I needed. Otherwise, I would not have been armed with the skills and confidence necessary to enter the workplace. Had it not been for the advantages and parental support I was given, I would never have been able to advance in the work field as I have. Later on, I never would have been able to achieve degrees in Psychology and Computer Sciences. If that had not happened, I, like many of my classmates, would have grown frustrated with learning and given up.

I am now writing this book for the parents, guardians, and educators of kids like me. I am writing to ensure that they can ask the questions they need to ask and support their children and students in the way that they need and deserve to be supported. In doing so, I can show such parents, guardians, and educators what they need to do to help their students acquire their diplomas and go out into the world with the knowledge, motivation, and confidence they need to succeed.

Chapter 1:

What Is Culturally

Responsive Teaching?

Importance for Educational System

We live in a changing world; one made up of infinitely varied individuals of different ethnic, cultural, and socio-economic backgrounds. Uniformity is neither a rule nor a reasonable expectation to have when walking into a given space, such as a school. In the past, it used to be both. This means that the education system that was developed in the past—and that we largely continue to use today—was created for a uniform audience hailing from the same kind of background. It was tailored to primarily meet the educational needs of white, middle-class students. Now that classrooms have become more diverse, though, the education system in place is no longer working as it should. It has become unable to meet the needs of the student body within the system simply because it no longer understands what those needs are. It is able to meet the educational needs of some students but not others. This creates a distinct and unfair imbalance within the education system. Therefore, the education system itself needs to change. It needs to be adapted and evolved so that it can understand and address the needs of each and every student within the system. This is where culturally responsive teaching comes in.

Culturally responsive teaching dictates that students' cultural references must be included in all aspects of the learning process. Culture can be defined as the beliefs, values, languages, symbols, and artifacts that are a part of a given society (University of Minnesota, 2016). It can also be defined as a set of values, beliefs, and practices that are grounded in the shared experiences and history of a group of people (Caffarrella, 2010). The traditional education model at hand focuses on a hierarchical relationship between a student and a teacher that come from the same background (Burnham, 2020).

In this model, a teacher from a white, middle-class background might teach the works of authors such as

Charles Dickens or J.D. Salinger to his students. Thinking solely from the perspective of his background, he might forget to include authors from other, more diverse backgrounds in his curriculum, such as Toni Morrison, Maya Angelou, or Sandra Cisneros. This is problematic because when such authors are excluded from the curriculum, students from diverse backgrounds might feel that they are excluded. They might have difficulty connecting to course material that does not resonate with their life experience, background, or perspectives. Unable to make this connection, they might do poorly in class compared to their classmates.

Culturally responsive teaching does not make this mistake. A teacher who embraces this teaching model will typically recognize that traditional texts, like *Oliver Twist* by Charles Dickens, are great but aren't the only great works out there. The teacher will therefore make an effort to include the works of other authors in his class, like Toni Morrison. This way, the teacher can ensure that different students feel a greater sense of connection to the course material and thus become a greater part of the class. This is just one example of one strategy educators can use to adopt culturally responsive teaching methods. There are other strategies they can adopt depending on what class they are teaching and what subject matter they are covering.

The critical thing about all these strategies is that they address the realities that the students of the 21st century live in. They come with a wide range of benefits for students, teachers, classrooms, and, ultimately, society itself. One of these benefits is that they strengthen students' sense of identity. Another is that it promotes inclusivity and equality in the classroom by leveling the playing field for all. It promotes greater understanding between students of different ethical, cultural, and socio-economic backgrounds. It introduces students to other cultures by having them read the works of authors from different cultures. It also supports critical thinking skills in students, especially once they grow more invested in the course materials they are learning. Simply put, it makes students more eager to learn and able to achieve the success that they need in their academic careers. This helps educators maintain calmer, more peaceful, and more engaged classrooms and learning environments. It makes it easier for them to do the job that they chose: helping students to grow, develop and go on to lead successful lives. Adopting culturally responsive teaching methods makes teachers and educators more successful, as their level of success is determined by their own students' levels of success. It also makes their day-to-day job far easier than it otherwise would have been and eliminates a prime source of frustration from their lives.

Before delving into what culturally responsive teaching strategies are and how they can be implemented, let us explore why this teaching method is so important. We've seen why this method is essential for educators. So, why is it significant for parents and guardians? Why is it vital for all students, not just those from different backgrounds? In other words, what are the actual benefits of culturally responsive teaching in both the short and the long term?

Importance for Parents and Guardians

Though this might sound rather curious, culturally responsive teaching is just as important for parents and guardians as it is for students. This is because the methodology increases parents' and guardians' involvement in their children's education, much in the same way that it increases students' participation in class. Culturally diverse students come from culturally diverse families. These parents and guardians want their children to get equal opportunities at school, truly learn, and go on to become successful adults. To that end, many parents and guardians become engaged in their children's school. They attend parent-teacher conferences, participate in PTA meetings, help with their kids' homework, etc. Parent engagement is very important for students' academic success. Studies show that it impacts student behavior and raises students' level of academic achievement. It also lowers students' likelihood of engaging in unhealthy behaviors that could harm their academic success, such as substance use (Centers for Disease Control, 2021).

A school that embraces a culturally responsive teaching methodology increases parent engagement. It makes culturally diverse parents and guardians a greater part of the education system, just as it makes their students more engaged in their classes and school life. It creates an environment at school where parents, guardians, and students feel comfortable and welcome.

An example of this is seen in Fraser Elementary School (Johnson, 2007). This was a school that was known for its high transiency rates, poor attendance records, discipline problems among its students, and overall declining condition of its school building. After a new principal was assigned to Fraser Academy, specific changes began taking place. The school principal instituted multicultural assemblies at school, for instance. She started holding staff development workshops for teachers and educators. She actively worked as a community advocate to create changes to the school that would make it a safer, more secure place for students. As a result, parents and guardians whose kids attended Fraser Academy began to feel more welcome on campus. They also began to feel that they were respected a great deal more by the school and its teachers. All of this helped increase parent engagement at Fraser Academy a great deal. This, in turn, resulted in lower transiency rates, better attendance records, fewer discipline problems among students, and an improved and safer learning environment (Johnson, 2007).

The culturally responsive teaching methods that Fraser Academy adopted made parents and guardians a more significant part of their children's school. Parents became active parts of their children's academic lives. This positively impacted students' behavior and performance. It allowed them to get better grades, participate more in class and do better academically. These are things that all parents and guardians want. Culturally responsive teaching methods also increased parents' and guardians' satisfaction with their children's schools. It increased their sense of self-satisfaction too, this being a direct result of their feeling more welcome and respected on campus. The more respected and welcome parents and guardians feel on campus, the more engaged they will be in their children's schools and education. Take what happened at Coleman Elementary School as an example (Johnson, 2007). The new principal at this school instituted an open-door policy on arrival. She did so because she believed parents and guardians should be a big part of their children's academic lives and feel that they belonged there. To that end, she instituted workshops for parents and guardians and recruited a number of them as part of the school's on-site decision-making team. If parents and guardians came to her with a particular problem, she took their concerns and opinions to the appropriate teacher and spoke to them on their behalf. She provided parents and guardians with the support and help they needed. She made an effort to hire diverse community members as part of the school staff. This ensured that the community, the children at her school, and their parents and guardians came from was represented and that their voices were heard. Over time, parents and guardians came to believe and feel that they were part of the school community and started to actively take part in the school. This affected their children's behavior, as well as the way they approached their classes and homework.

Based on these examples, it can be said that culturally responsive teaching aims to do several things where parents and guardians are concerned. First, it commits to involving and consulting parents and guardians in school decisions that impact the quality of education their children receive. This is why the methodology gives parents and guardians the opportunity to review school curriculum, for instance. Culturally responsive teaching incorporates students' cultural knowledge into the curriculum, as we've already seen. Schools need the support of their district officials to implement multicultural curriculums (Johnson, 2007). But they also can benefit significantly from any help parents and guardians can provide them with. By reviewing their children's curriculum, parents and guardians can provide schools and educators with invaluable feedback as to what might be improved, expanded on, and added to. Hence the Coleman principal instituted an open-door policy and held workshops for parents and guardians. Parents can have a similar impact by meeting with educators to discuss how the education system in place or even the school grounds can be improved. This gives parents and guardians a thorough understanding of their children's strengths and weaknesses. It also helps them to understand what they can do to help their children improve and how they could support them in the areas they struggle in. Essentially culturally responsive teaching methods try to create a school culture where parents and guardians and educators are parents and guardians, working together to increase their students' level of success (Rodriguez et al., 2008).

Importance for Students

We've already established that culturally responsive teaching increases student engagement in class and thus helps them excel in their academic careers. However, this is not the only reason why this methodology is so important for students. Culturally responsive teaching has a wide array of benefits. For one, the inclusion of diverse backgrounds and personalities allows students to view and understand matters from each other's perspective—something they otherwise might not have been able to do. This opens up new avenues of thought for them and fosters critical thinking (ColumbiaLearn, 2021). At the same time, it creates a safe space within the classroom, where students feel welcome, comfortable, and that they belong. This is the kind of environment that empowers students and allows them to freely ask questions, without fear or hesitation. Students are able to do this in such an environment because the attitude their teacher has created conveys the "it is my responsibility to help you if I can" message (ColumbiaLearn, 2021). Teachers and educators who are able to convey this message effectively change their students' understanding of errors and mistakes. If students consider errors a sign that they lack proficiency in a given subject, then they will be hesitant to ask the questions they need to ask to fix that error.

As a result, they likely will not be able to correct mistakes and gain proficiency. If students view errors as a natural part of the learning process, then they will be far more likely to ask questions when they have them. In doing so, they will be better able to understand the subject matter before them, fix mistakes, and in time gain proficiency. Being able to do so, though, is contingent on the formation of a safe place, through culturally responsive teaching. These safe spaces are constructed with positive, encouraging attitudes on the teacher's part. They, therefore, foster positivity and a constructive approach among students. Furthermore, they make students feel more validated and encourage teamwork and collaboration among them by increasing their understanding of one another. In essence, they become the kind of environment where every student has the same learning opportunities, which enables teachers and educators to find talents that might have otherwise gone unnoticed. They create a shared understanding where each and every student can truly thrive and achieve success.

You may be wondering how precisely instructors can create a safe space for students. There are preliminary steps, which can be expanded upon further, that culturally responsive teachers and educators should bear in mind to create the safe space they need to help their students succeed (Sandoval, 2020). These are as follows:

- Setting the tone for their class

- Co-Constructing class expectations and norms with their students

- Acknowledging differences

- Focusing on building community and rapport among students

- Responding directly to harm

Instructors should set the tone for their classes at the very beginning of the school year. This tone should clearly prioritize equity, diversity, and inclusion in the class. These things should be embedded within the course material, as well as the way in which class interactions and discussions are managed. That being said, instructors should refrain from making assumptions about different students' understandings, experiences, and perspectives. This is where co-constructing expectations and norms with students come into play. Co-constructing expectations and standards means asking students plainly and directly about their learning experiences thus far. It means having them talk to you and each other about these things openly and honestly. When have they had positive learning experiences in class? What have these experiences been like and why were they positive for them? Have there been any times when they felt like their learning experiences were not working for them? Have there been any times when they felt they needed something different from their classroom, classmates, or teachers? If so, what was it that they needed? In having such discussions with students, instructors can create the kind of learning environment that best understand and respond to their needs. Thus, they can truly support their students on the way to success. Another way they can do this is by acknowledging students' differences. Contrary to what some might think, ignoring people's differences does not generate a more equal learning environment. Instead, it sweeps those differences under the rug, thereby making people feel invisible or that their needs aren't being met. When instructors openly acknowledge differences though they bring the experiences, perspectives, and worldviews of different individuals into the safe space they are creating. They make students feel seen and validated, allow them to understand one another to a greater extent, and invite them to engage more with their class. This is something that directly feeds into the next thing that instructors need to do to create safe spaces in class: building a community and establishing rapport among students.

Building a community within a class can be vital for students' success and well-being. When an instructor focuses on generating an understanding between students, they help them to feel more connected to one another. Instructors can further reinforce this feeling of connectedness by doing team-building exercises and giving group assignments to their students. When students feel that they belong to the community that you are founding in class, they inevitably feel more connected to and invested in that class. They also feel far more supported. Building a community of care in class means that students can turn to each other for support when they need it. Of course, instructors must be there for their students when they need help. But forming a community stops that being solely your responsibility as an instructor. Instead, the burden becomes a shared one among all students participating in that class. This increases the level of trust among students. It must be remembered, though, that trust can be hard to earn and easy to break. A sure way to break students' trust—in the class, in each other, or in you as the instructor—is to ignore harm. Students of diverse backgrounds can sometimes hurt one another, intentionally or without meaning to, for lack of understanding. Instructors can cause hurt to their students without meaning to as well. When this happens, some instructors might try to shut down the incident or argument. They might try to move on in an attempt to solve the situation. Moving on without acknowledging the hurt that was done, however, can be incredibly damaging. It can break students' trust in the class and their instructor. It can disrupt the safe space within the class and create fractures in the community that has been established. The better and understandably harder thing to do would be to acknowledge whatever hurt has been done, rather than trying to move on. This does not mean that instructors must know the absolute right thing to say. It just means that they should acknowledge that pain has been caused to a student and a group of students. The instructor can then ask for some time to consider the event so that they can find the best way to approach the situation. They can also hold calm, open dialogues with their students about what they think can be done and what their points of view are. It is clear that culturally responsive teaching requires building trust between students and instructors. This necessitates establishing a certain kind of language and dialogue in class, one that students will respond to. Instructors can best do this by taking care to understand the context and norms that are prevalent in the language they use as they teach a class. If a teacher is using language that discounts the context that a student is unfamiliar with, that student might have a difficult time connecting to and understanding the course material. They might also come to feel that their instructor does not really understand them and thus find it harder to trust them. The language that instructors use must also be person-centered. This means that instructors should be mindful of their students' individuality, personhood, and dignity as they engage with them. Students will be far more likely to engage in class when they feel that their individuality is respected, much in the same way their parents and guardians engage more in their children's school lives when they feel welcome and respected on campus.

Of course, the safe spaces and communities that instructors establish might look a little different in in-person classes than they do in online classes. Earning students' trust and providing them with the inclusive space they deserve requires taking some additional measures. The first of these is ensuring that the course materials and assignments presented to students are as clear as humanly possible. The second is embracing a universal design. This is something that traditional educational methods have largely failed at for many years. Historically speaking, educational materials have primarily been made for the "average person". Because the people who were preparing these materials were usually white, middle-class, heterosexual, cis-gendered men, they considered people like them to be the "average person". This, however, is an incorrect assumption. The majority of the people in the world aren't white, middle-class, cis-gendered, or heterosexual. When people of different, diverse backgrounds are made to engage in course materials that only take this definition of "the average man" as an example, they inevitably disengage from the class. If the course materials presented to students took more diverse "average persons" as their examples though, this would cease to be a problem. This is why embracing a universal design is crucial for student success. Online classes tend to be heavy on the visual side, with video lectures, presentations, documentaries, and more. These visual materials have a universal understanding of the average person. So too should any written materials be presented to students. Only then can students really begin learning and connecting with the subjects they are being taught.

There are two other factors that culturally responsive online classes should bear in mind: accessibility and the digital divide. Accessibility is something that some teachers and educators might not consider until and unless the school they belong to explicitly asks them to. A culturally responsive teacher, however, should not need to be asked. They should already have closed captioning or voice recordings of lectures ready to use on the platforms they upload their course materials to. They must be prepared to accommodate the needs of students with different learning methods—e.g., visual and aural—as well as those with disabilities, such as deaf students. Similarly, they must be conscious of the digital divide that exists today. True, most students these days have a computer or phone and are able to connect to the internet. However, not everyone has an unlimited data plan to keep watching hour-long lectures or tablets to easily read PDFs. If a student is not able to do their work because the class does not take the digital divide they are facing into account, then they will naturally struggle in that class. They will do worse, academically speaking, compared to their classmates who are easily able to access the provided PDFs on their brand-new tablets. If their needs and abilities are taken into account in online classes though, their academic performance will improve by leaps and bounds.

Chapter 2:

Why Is Culturally

Responsive Teaching So

Important?

It is blatantly apparent that culturally responsive teaching is incredibly important for educators, parents, guardians, and students. This is because it takes into things that traditional teaching methods do not. It eliminates and makes up for the failure of traditional methods and gives all students an equal opportunity to excel. In order to better understand why this is, though, we must first establish just how culturally responsive teaching differs from traditional methods. Why is traditional education not a good fit for everyone? Why does it fail to inspire a culturally diverse classroom? How, precisely, do the differences between students— be they socioeconomic, language-related, or cultural— prevent students from fully engaging with their courses? How do traditional teaching methods let some students down and cause them to drop out?

What Are Traditional Teaching Methods Anyways?

Traditional learning consists of learning methods that were created for a very specific reason: to prepare students to join the existing workforce of the colonial period. In the colonial period, the traditional student was expected to go into some kind of clerical job after completing his education. In his new position, he was meant to obey whatever direction and orders his seniors and employers gave him without asking questions and without hesitation or objection. As such, traditional learning methods were designed to discourage asking questions (Flygare et al., 2021). They focused on rote learning and memorization and centered, unequivocally, on memorization. It did not matter if a student truly learned the subject matter he was being taught. What mattered was that he followed orders, took notes, and memorized what he needed to. If he wrote something down incorrectly, he would be penalized for it. This penalization would take the form of lower grades in class and during exams. Said student would similarly be punished if he refrained from taking notes in class. Traditional teaching methods, then, completely disregarded practical utility over rote learning. In the past decades, it even went as far as to eliminate and exclude trade job training from the system. School budgets for automotive, electrical, carpentry, plumbing, and other skill-based trade training were promptly cut. This deeply impacted culturally diverse students whose various skill-based talents were thus made to go unrecognized. As you might imagine, this situation took a toll on students' level of self-confidence and still does so today. Take shop class as an example. Shop classes used to be part of many public and private schools. These days, though, it is pretty difficult to come across one, as schools have chosen to eliminate it from the curriculum. This is detrimental to society.

The primary reason for this is that the focus traditional teaching puts on standardized testing and college admission levels—which will be discussed at length later on—caused courses like shop class to become undervalued. Schools began to evaluate their level of success by how high their students' exam scores were and which colleges they were getting into (Generation T, 2021). They started viewing skill-based trades, which are developed in classes like shop class, as unimportant. They reasoned that the money spent on shop class could be better spent elsewhere. Thus, shop class was cut out of most curriculums permanently. There are three problems with this reasoning. The first is that it damages students' self-confidence as previously mentioned because it means their talents go unrecognized. When students' talents are overlooked, they become unlikely to develop them. When students do not develop skills that could lead to a future career and source of income for them, they lose out on the successful future that they could have. Not only that, but they become disinterested in school and become more likely to drop out.

The second problem is that parents and guardians believe their children should choose their own career paths. But how can children make accurate decisions if they do not experience a variety of different career options? How can children choose specific careers for themselves, if they are not made aware of the paths that are around them? The third and final problem is that classes like shop class do a phenomenal job of teaching children certain scientific concepts in action. In shop class, students see and observe the concepts that keep motors running and bridges standing up in action. They also learn how to run businesses that are based on skill-based crafts. The elimination of such classes, then, prevents students from learning by doing in a lot of different ways. This is sadly in keeping with the way that traditional teaching methods work. Traditional teaching makes no room for creative thinking, visualization, out-of-the-box thinking, and rational thinking (Morrison, 2019). Because of this, it bleeds students' creativity, innovation, and critical thinking skills right out of them.

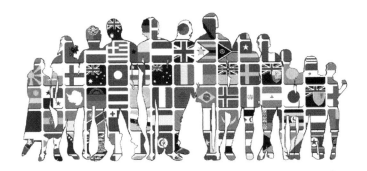

Traditional teaching methods made sense for the times that they were founded. After all, the job market that students would be going into required employees who would not ask questions and obey whatever orders were given to them, at least for the most part. However, the needs of the job market have changed substantially in the 21st century. What worked in the past no longer works for the current economic system and the society we live in. Most students cannot achieve success following graduation by adhering to traditional learning methods. In fact, some are even forced to drop out of the education system entirely when traditional learning methods are incessantly forced on them. Traditional teaching methods fail to help students stand on their own two feet, build up their self-confidence and earn a good living in the future. There are several reasons for this. The first is that traditional learning methods prevent students from focusing on what they should learn. Discouraged from asking questions, students never wonder how the things they are learning will benefit them in the future. They never ask questions like, "Why am I being introduced to this subject?" or "How will this knowledge help me later?" (Morrison, 2019). This means that most students go through whatever course materials are presented to them without trying or intending to truly understand them. Their only aim, under the yoke of traditional teaching, is to memorize those materials. They focus on passing their various quizzes and tests. In doing so, they fail to grasp the essence of their courses and thus lose out on valuable information.

The second reason why traditional teaching methods fail is that they focus on theoretical knowledge rather than skill-based knowledge (Morrison, 2019). What this means is that the "learn by doing" ideology is not embraced by traditional teaching. For instance, a lot of chemistry teachers and educators teach theoretical concepts without having students practice what they learn through experimentation. Students thus do not get to observe that which they learn in action. Neither do they get to directly engage with it. This kind of theoretical focus actively hinders the development of innovation, observation skills, critical thinking skills, and out-of-the-box thinking abilities that are so important for students and educators today. Some schools of course recognize this and would like to adopt skill-based teaching methods. However, they often fear or are hesitant to change their learning methods because they lack the resources to do so. In the case of the chemistry class example, for instance, changing learning methods would require creating or using a lab and getting lab equipment. This can be a rather expensive endeavor and schools might therefore balk at the idea, used to theoretical knowledge-based teaching methods as they are.

Cultural Barriers: Another reason why traditional teaching methods do not work is that they do not explain the importance of education to the students that they are trying to serve. This is something that is very much in keeping with the ideology that traditional teaching is based on. Remember, this method was founded on the idea that future employees should not question their superiors. Their superiors or employers, then, should not have to explain whatever reasoning they have for the decisions they make to their employees. The student-teacher relationship in the framework of traditional teaching is meant to mimic future employee-manager/superior relationships. Given that, why should teachers and educators have to explain their reasonings for teaching certain subjects to their students? Why should the school or education system—a stand-in for the future job market or company the student will go in—explain the importance of education to students? This is the logic that runs through traditional teaching methods. This is why this methodology focuses on getting through a syllabus on time, rather than paying attention to how well students learn what they are being taught. It is why it focuses on students' exam grades, which in truth give false impressions of how well students are doing in school. It fails to impart the value of education to students, who therefore do not pay attention in class and just try to get through classes without really digesting their lessons. Cultivating successful students who go on to become successful adults in our day and time requires a shift in focus. This means that teaching methods should focus on how education impacts students' individual lives, society as a whole, and the national economy. Seeing as the needs of our society and national economy have changed, traditional teaching methods aren't able to do any of these things.

One side-effect of this situation is that the value society has placed on education has decreased. Over time, teaching has become an undervalued occupation, despite how crucial it is for our society and economy. There is a reason, after all, that most teachers are paid very little. This, in turn, has resulted in fewer and fewer people going into teaching. Consequently, the quality of teachers in our current education system has gone down as well and teaching has become highly commercialized. A lot of teachers and educators go into the industry with the goal of moving to cushier positions, or institutions and, thus, making more money. The education system as defined by traditional teaching methods is therefore made up of less experienced teachers. This means that many of the people we entrust with our children's futures are below average in their academic careers. They are in the positions they are in because there is a distinct lack of qualified teachers and educators. In the absence of qualified teachers, individuals that have the necessary certificates and degrees are able to become teachers, even if they are not of the quality society needs them to be.

Teachers and educators who land in their positions because of such vacuums or in pursuit of loftier positions are not able to evoke students' interest in the subject matters that they teach. Teachers and educators who cannot get their students interested in their classes cannot be considered good teachers, no matter how much of an expert they are in their fields. This is because students who are disinterested in their classes will become bored and not learn anything they are supposed to learn. Of course, this is not always entirely the teachers' fault. The existing discrepancy between the number of students and the number of teachers and educators in the education system is also to blame. Studies show that the ideal student-to-teacher ratio for the optimal learning environment is 20:1 (Morrison, 2019). The current average ratio, however, is 60:1. Let us say that a teacher has 60 students to teach and only 60 minutes, per class, to do it. This means that he can devote a single minute to each student, max, per class. Such a teacher will neither be able to answer students' questions properly nor will he be able to make sure that they truly understand what they are being taught. Teachers' jobs are made ever more difficult by the perpetual lack of resources they're always facing. Schools and even societies often fail to provide teachers with the resources they need to provide for the future of our societies. Because of this, many teachers try to purchase the supplies their students need using their own salaries. This unfortunately proves unsustainable rather quickly. This being the case, it is no wonder that the teachers who stick to culturally responsive teaching methods focus on speed and grades over the quality of learning. These teachers and educators focus on finishing their classes on time and what their students' exam grades are. These are the parameters by which they are judged.

The problem is this kind of focus fails to take into account the many different factors that might prevent students from performing well in school. Students, for instance, might be dealing with psychological issues, such as depression. They might be dealing with physical abuse or bullying. They might find that they are discouraged from asking questions and thus have trouble understanding their courses. They might find it difficult to speak up in class because they are more introverted compared to their classmates. They might be dealing with challenging family situations that divert their focus or make it hard for them to focus on their work. All of these factors can impact students' grades and academic performance. Traditional teaching methods also do not take students' varying backgrounds and differences into account. For example, some students might be first-generation learners, meaning they are the first in their families to pursue an education. Others might be faster learners than others. Some may have trouble grasping specific subjects, like math or history. Others might not have environments at home that are conducive to learning and studying. For instance, a student's parents and guardians have to work until very late at night and there is no one to take care of him at home. This student might, therefore, have to do a variety of chores when he gets home or even take care of his younger siblings and this would leave him with very little time to study. The fact of the matter is traditional learning methods take none of these things into account. Culturally responsive teaching methods, on the other hand, do. This is why culturally responsive methods are crucial to ensuring students' current and future success.

Barriers to Learning

Cultural Barriers

There can be several different barriers to learning, as has already been pointed out. This is because students come from all different kinds of backgrounds and situations. As each of them are unique individuals, leading individual lives, they might have unique barriers that could prevent them from doing well in school. In order to understand how culturally responsive teaching can help with these barriers—and how traditional education does not—we must first understand what said barriers are. We must begin by grasping what leads students to say, "These are not my life experiences. Why should I care about this subject?" The socio-cultural barriers that students face within the education system can be summed up as follows (UNESCO, 2019):

- Their cultural and ethnic background and contributions to various fields (e.g., history, literature, etc.) aren't recognized in the curriculum.

- Their cultural and ethnic identities aren't reflected in the curriculum or course materials.

- Certain beliefs exist within the culture they belong to prohibit or restrict the access of certain individuals, such as girls or children with disabilities, to education.

- The culture that they are a part of either does not recognize the actual value of education or undervalues it.

Cultural barriers to education can exist on multiple fronts: at school, among students, among parents and guardians and families, and in entire communities. For example, some parents and guardians might think that an academic education is not all that valuable. Their communities might hold beliefs that make pursuing an education an unsuitable practice for girls or children with disabilities. Similarly, cultural barriers might exist among teachers. A teacher might, consciously or not, hold certain beliefs about the learning capabilities of children from certain kinds of cultural, socio-economic, ethnic, and religious backgrounds. All of this can prevent students from attending school and cause some that do attend to feel unwelcome in school and therefore drop out. Some students might feel unwelcome in their own communities and culture because they go to school, which might cause them to struggle academically and again, drop out. This is why it is incredibly important to dismantle and mitigate beliefs about the importance of education. It is why creating inclusive, equitable education systems that welcome is absolutely vital. Doing so, however, is no easy task, especially since beliefs about education and its suitability for some kinds of students must be dismantled without disrespecting or undervaluing the culture those students come from. To achieve this challenging task, we must grasp that cultural barriers are fostered by cultural factors that are embedded into the fabric of different groups' cultural identities (Caffarrella, 2010). In other words, we must understand that cultural barriers are rooted in cultural beliefs. For example, if one community holds certain negative beliefs about another community of different ethnicity, they might be reluctant to send their children to the same school. The children that do attend school might adopt their parents' and guardians' views about other ethnicities. As such a general air of distrust and even hostility may reign in school, just as it does among parents and guardians. Some communities don't believe that women and girls should be educated. Their cultural beliefs speak out against their going to school.

This is a significant cultural barrier to overcome where education is concerned, not the least because the student body makeup of schools has significantly changed over the years. Between 1998 and 2008, for instance, the percentage of white students attending US public schools went from 68% to 55% (Sau Hou Chang, 2013). At the same time, the percentage rate of Hispanic students attending the same schools rose from 11% to 22%. Teachers and educators trying to educate their students must keep these potential cultural differences in mind as they teach if they wish to overcome the cultural barriers that stand in their way. They must recognize, for instance, that the one-size fits all education system that used to work in the past no longer does. They must recognize that teachers, students, schools, parents and guardians, and communities might hold beliefs that could become barriers to education and thus work to dismantle them. These barriers must be dismantled both on school grounds and outside of school. Teachers and educators who want to break down cultural barriers in their classes can begin by learning other cultures' values, traditions, ways of communicating, contributions (historical, literary, etc.), learning styles, and relationship patterns. They can then use what they learn to develop multicultural and engaging educational methods. Take the story of one teacher who had to get her students interested in poetry. Instead of diving into the works of long-dead poets, this teacher recognized that rap was a form of poetry. She also recognized that rap was a big part of certain communities' culture, as well as popular culture. So, she had her second-grade students bring in bits of rap lyrics to class and had them perform them. She then used these lyrics to discuss poetry tools such as onomatopoeia, rhyme schemes, and alliteration. Thus, she overcame a potential cultural barrier that created the impression poetry was only accessible to certain cultural groups and not others.

Another thing teachers and educators can do to overcome cultural barriers is to include cultural and ethnic diversity in their curriculum. They can do this by analyzing how ethnic groups and their contributions are present in mass media and popular culture. When they encounter controversy, they can deal with it by studying diverse individuals and groups. They can contextualize contemporary and historic issues within different classes, races, ethnicities, and genders. Thus, they can incorporate different perspectives into their lessons. They can further accomplish this by making sure to include images of people of different cultural backgrounds in the visual materials that they use. At the same time, they can keep communicating openly with their diverse students. Thanks to this they can reflect their cultural values and learning behaviors. They can use all that they learn to build communities both in and outside of class. They can use their students' own experiences to expand their intellectual horizons, improve their academic performance and design communal learning environments that would be beneficial to all. In doing so, they could dismantle preconceived ideas about learning, education, and people of different backgrounds, all of which can be barriers to education.

There are plenty of things that teachers can do to dismantle cultural barriers to education outside of the classroom and even school. The same is true for school officials and local authorities. The first is to kick off campaigns to raise enrollment awareness among communities. These campaigns can do wonders in gradually breaking down socio-cultural barriers to schooling, so long as they correctly understand and respect the cultures that they are speaking to. Such campaigns need strong advocates from civil society. This means that teachers and educators need to band together with education officers, parents and guardians, families, children, local authorities, parents and guardians' organizations and religions, and local leaders. Only by working together can all these people change various communities' minds and perspectives. Take what happened in Tanzania as an example. In 2017, a campaign was launched to address gender issues such as child marriage and early pregnancy. 20 local leaders, including highly respected imams, participated in the campaign. Thus, they were able to change the widely held beliefs of many members of their community. While this was not a campaign that was directly related to education, this successful campaign is a great example of what such dedicated programs can achieve. It must be said, though, that these campaigns become infinitely more effective when they are paired with local and national media campaigns. Media, by its nature, has an extensive reach. So too do the many social media platforms out there. Because of this, media and social media campaigns can be invaluable in disseminating information on the value of education and dismantling barriers that stand in the way. A good example of this is a media campaign that was launched in Nepal. This campaign widely shared the stories of children with disabilities attending school and showed how well they were doing. In doing so, they both discredited beliefs that such children would not be able to do well in school and raised awareness of their right to an education.

Physical and media—social media campaigns are essential tools for disrupting cultural barriers to schooling. They are made much more effective, though, when they are accompanied by policy changes in schools. If a school is uncertain as to how it could alter its policies to create a more inclusive learning environment, it can begin local policy dialogues with the communities it serves. In doing so, it can better understand the cultural barriers to learning and see how its policies aren't addressing and solving them. In other words, it can learn to see avenues it otherwise would have been blind to and begin rooting its policies in local concerns. It can ensure that this happens by including more diverse voices in the decision-making process where policies are concerned. This would promote the participation of the part of different communities in the decision-making process at schools and begin reforming existing barriers to schooling. Involving parents and guardians of more diverse cultural backgrounds in organizations like the PTA would achieve the same result. So too would hiring teachers and educators of a more diverse backgrounds.

Language Barriers

Language barriers can prevent both student involvement in class and parents' and guardians' involvement in their child's education. We've grown used to thinking that everybody speaks English these days. However, take a walk through a crowded city like New York or poke your head into one of the large schools in your district and you'll find this is not really the case. There are a great many students in our current education system who either do not speak English or do not speak it very well yet. These students are learning English as a second language, meaning their native language is something completely different, like French, Chinese or Spanish. Between the years 2012 and 2013, there were 4.85 million students who were English language learners in the US education system. By 2016, this figure had doubled and there were about 10 million such students (Mungia, 2017). This number has only increased in 2022 and will no doubt continue to do so. Students who are learning English as a second language have a unique barrier to contend with. Learning English as a second language is hard, for one thing. As such, if these students do not receive the proper help that they need, they will struggle academically. After all, how can they hope to do well in math class, for example, if they cannot understand what the teacher is talking about? At the same time, these students may find assimilating into the new culture they have found themselves in without undercutting or demeaning their native language and culture to be challenging. Students having difficulties like this can have quite a difficult time in class if certain accommodations aren't made for their language barrier.

One accommodation that can help students to do well in school is to adopt a bilingual teaching method. Being bilingual means being able to speak two different languages. Bilingual education is a method that actively enforces and fosters this ability. Bilingual education methods work in this way: Schools have their teachers and continue with regular classes, conducted in English on the one side. On the other, they have them do one of two things. Either they have teachers and educators teach English as a second language to the students that need it, or they choose to have classes in another language to support these students academically. What this second language ends up being is typically left up to local authorities. There are a couple of methods schools can embrace as they deliver a bilingual education to their students. These methods are known as immersion, transitional bilingual education, and developmental or maintenance bilingual education (Mungia, 2017).

The immersion method is all about immersing students in the English language. In this model, classes are exclusively taught in English. However, the teachers and educators teaching these classes take care to use simple, even rudimentary language in class. This way they make things easier to understand for their students.

The transitional bilingual education method, on the other hand, couples English language instruction with instruction in students' native languages. Say a student's native language is Spanish and he is having a tough time in biology. The biology teacher in this case would teach the course in English, then in Spanish so that the student can understand precisely what's being taught and discussed. This way language and culture gaps standing before the student would be bridged.

The last method, developmental or maintenance bilingual education, entails building on students' native language while having them study English as well. This ensures that they do not become disconnected from their own language and progress in English at the same time. Of course, for these methods to work, schools and teachers must ensure that students are assigned qualified teachers in all their classes. If teachers and educators are not skilled in the languages and subject matters they are teaching, then the students will not be learning much. The lack of a qualified educator will become a learning barrier for them. So too will be given inferior instruction. The instruction that a non-native speaker is given must be on the same level as that given to a native speaker for this to not become a barrier. At the same time, teachers teaching non-native speakers must be given enough time to go through the curriculum and ensure that their students understand the subject matter. They must hold their classes in facilities that match the quality of the facilities—be they school buildings or classrooms—of native speakers. Finally, non-native speakers' knowledge must be assessed using qualified instruments and by qualified instructors. Otherwise, no one will be able to get an accurate picture of how that student is doing academically, how much progress they have made, and what challenges they might be facing.

While bilingual education methods can be instrumental in helping students to learn, there is some controversy around them. People have argued against bilingual teaching on both political grounds—which will not be discussed in this book—and pedagogical grounds. The pedagogical argument against bilingual education is that learning two languages at the same time can confuse students and lower their proficiency in both languages. There is also some worry that teaching English as a second language interferes with students' native languages and that bilingual education makes assimilating harder for students and thus causes segregation among the student body. Such arguments, however, are inaccurate. If they were not, then students who grew up in foreign countries, like Germany, for instance, and learned English as a second language in their school would never be able to become proficient in English. This is a fact that most studies examining bilingual education recognize. These studies further show that there has not been any objective evidence proving the arguments made against this educational method. This is why the US Department of Education maintains that developing students' native languages in class does not interfere with their ability to learn

English. The Department of Education further recognizes that bilingual education methods improve students' cognitive and communication skills. It understands that the methodology fosters respect among native and non-native speaker students and enhances non-native speakers' learning ability and future job prospects (Mungia, 2017).

There are, of course, other things teachers can do to support students who are non-native speakers during their academic journeys. They begin doing so by learning to pronounce their names correctly (Network Support, 2019). This might seem like a relatively simple thing, but you'd be surprised at what a great difference it can make. A lot of students who are learning English as a second language have names that may sound unique. When teachers mispronounce these names, they unwittingly make students feel like outsiders. This makes them less confident in class and less likely to participate. Put simply, it is something that can easily turn into a learning barrier. When students' names are pronounced correctly, however, teachers and educators are able to win their trust and build rapport with them. This helps create the safe learning environments teachers want in class, which in turn makes students more likely to ask questions, such as when they do not understand a particular word or phrase. Another method that can help overcome language barriers like this is using the buddy system. Teachers and educators can pair non-native English speakers with native English speakers. The native speakers can then act as a translator for their buddies, enabling them to participate in class to a greater extent. This would also increase interaction between native and non-native speakers, thereby allowing them to form better, more trusting relationships.

Using various visuals in class can also be very effective in overcoming language barriers. Supplementing written class materials and assignments, as well as lectures, with sketches, photos, gestures, audio or video clips and graphs can help students grasp lessons and concepts more quickly and easily. The ideal thing to do would be to prepare such materials before class. They can then be paired with hard-to-grasp concepts or even particularly difficult vocabulary words. The most important thing to keep in mind in a classroom setting though is that students who are learning English as a second language might be hesitant to ask for help when they need it, no matter how safe a space you create. They might be too embarrassed or shy to raise their hand and ask you to explain something in a crowded classroom. Given this, the most beneficial thing a teacher can do to help them overcome their language barriers is to encourage question-asking and check in with them from time to time (Network Support, 2019). Encouraging questions in class would help students feel more comfortable approaching you when they do not understand something. Checking in with them yourself would show them that you cared about them and give them the private space they need to ask their questions, without worrying about someone rolling their eyes at them.

As mentioned previously, language barriers do not just apply to students. They apply to parents and guardians as well and can lower parent participation in school and school activities a great deal. As we've seen, parent participation has a huge impact on students' academic performance. Parents who do not speak English well and do not really understand the written homework instructions will be unable to really help their kids with their homework, no matter how much they may want to. They will also be less likely to attend volunteer events, school fundraising activities, Parent Teacher Association (PTA) meetings, parent-teacher conferences, and even guidance counselor meetings (Baylor University, 2020). According to a report written in 2016, parents and guardians who either do not speak English or whose English is not very advanced are far less likely to participate in school activities than parents and guardians whose native language is English. There are several methods that teachers and schools can adopt to overcome this issue. One is to use a translator or interpreter at important meetings such as parent-teacher conferences and PTA meetings. These interpreters can actively translate what teachers and educators are saying. They can even translate the written documents and notices that are sent to students' homes. The same can be done with any meeting notes that are forwarded to them. Engaging the services of a professional translator can be costly, though, and not every school has the budget for it. Luckily, there are also apps teachers can use to do the exact same thing interpreters and translators do. Apps like Smore, TalkingPoints, and ClassDojo are just some examples. They would help parents and guardians understand what's going on in their children's classes a great deal more and thus allow them to be more engaged in their school lives.

One thing teachers and educators should bear in mind as they try to communicate with parents and guardians that aren't native speakers is that they should keep their language as direct, precise, and concise as possible. Removing idioms from speech patterns, along with figurative language and expressions is important as such things can be very confusing for non-native speakers. If you were to say, "It is raining cats and dogs out there," to someone who is just learning English, they would likely be baffled. The fact that they would be baffled, though, is not in any way indicative of their intelligence level. This is something that must be remembered when talking with such parents and guardians. Speaking to non-native speakers in a louder voice or with greater emphasis will not make them understand what's being said to them any better. It will only serve to frustrate them. Feeling that they are being disrespected, they would be likely to leave school grounds and stay away, unless they absolutely had to be there for some reason.

One final thing teachers and educators can do to overcome language barriers with parents and guardians and increase their involvement in school is to contact them for both positive and negative things. Teachers and educators would absolutely have to reach out to a child's parents and guardians when said child skips school. But they should also do so when that child improves remarkably in class and gets fantastic grades in his midterms. When teachers and schools do this, parents and guardians stop thinking of school involvement in solely negative terms. Instead, they begin to associate it with positive developments as well and, as with anything positive, they begin participating in their children's school lives more.

Socioeconomic Barriers

The socioeconomic status of students can greatly affect their academic progress and achievements. Socioeconomic status or SES refers to students' level of income, education attainment, financial security, and perception of their class or social status. At present, there is a massive disparity in educational resources and access between students from low-SES households and high-SES households (American Psychological Association, 2017). Studies show that children from low-SES households develop academic skills more slowly compared to children from high-SES households. This is because of a multitude of reasons. For one, children from low-SES families and communities deal with a great deal of physical and psychological stressors. For instance, they might witness the way their parents and guardians stress out about expenses and income, and this may adversely affect them, whether they realize it or not. These stressors can make focusing in class or on assignments rather difficult. Such children are, as a general rule, under-resourced compared to their contemporaries. Odds are they have fewer books to read at the house. They might not have computers or a stable internet connection at home, which would make doing their work incredibly difficult for them. Growing up, they are less likely to have experiences that encourage them to read and improve their cognitive and academic skills. Most students from low-SES communities are about 5 years behind their peers where their literacy rates are concerned. How could things be otherwise when they aren't given the resources and encouragement they need to improve this situation? The situation being what it is, it should be no surprise that low-income students have a higher drop-out rate than high-income students. In 2014, for instance, the dropout rate among low-income students was 11.6%. This rate was only 2.8% among students who came from high-income families.

Multiple studies and reviews show that children from low-SES communities both have higher dropout rates and do worse academically compared to other students. This situation is primarily caused by a lack of resources, which is a huge learning barrier for them. This lack of resources is not confined to their homes either. It also extends to the communities that they live in. Low-income communities, for instance, typically have fewer libraries within their neighborhoods. The libraries that do exist tend to open fewer times than libraries in other districts. They also usually have fewer and less qualified staff members tending to them. This initial learning barrier can be overcome through concentrated effort on the part of teachers, schools, and local (and national) policymakers. Schools, for instance, must recognize that their low-SES students need more, not less, resources in order to have equal opportunities academically. They must therefore allocate their resources differently and accordingly. Teachers and educators must recognize that students from low-SES situations are dealing with unique challenges and difficulties. They must therefore adjust their teaching methods and class expectations accordingly. Similarly, they must try to provide students with more resources themselves, if they observe that there is a need. Photocopying a book or sharing a PDF version of it with students in the class might be one way of doing this. If low-income students need to read these specific books for class but do not have the funds to allocate to this, then being provided with such a copy would be very appreciated, especially as it levels the playing field for all. Schools and school districts can take such measures even further by reaching out to the communities that these children come from. In beginning discussions within these communities, they can identify what resources are lacking and work to put policies in place to change that. They can re-examine the way they spend their funding. They can re-organize it to meet the needs of disadvantaged children and their families to a greater extent. They can have staff members in place to provide special assistance to those students who need it. Local authorities can do the same by allocating more resources to the lowest-performing schools in low-SES neighborhoods.

When teachers and educators and schools recognize that the reason some low SES students underperform is due to a lack of resources and not a lack of ability, they become able to dismantle a second, very big barrier to learning: mindset. Over time, students from low SES communities develop a kind of fixed mindset (Destin et al., 2019). They start attributing their underperformance at school not to their lack of resources but to their lack of ability. When teachers and educators recognize what the real problem is, however, they can begin to give their students the encouragement that they need to do better academically. They can help them to get access to necessary resources and show them their own potential. Being seen and recognized, encouraged, and appreciated can be an incredible motivator. It is something that can dismantle fixed mindsets over time and make students realize that they can be successful if they are given the tools they need to be able to do so.

Chapter 3:

How Do I Know If I Am a

Biased Teacher?

As uncomfortable as this might be to admit, we all have certain biases. Bias might be roughly defined as an inclination for or prejudice against someone or a particular group of people. Most of us pride ourselves on being fair. We like to think that we hold no biases.

But the problem is certain ideas, outlooks and yes, biases have been around for so long that they have become ingrained in our families, communities, the media we consume, and more. We absorb the messaging of all these things around us and internalize them to one degree or another, whether we realize it or not. Part of what we absorb and internalize is the biases that have become ingrained in the system we live in, the people we talk to, and the media we consume. What all this means is that it is entirely possible for teachers and educators—yes, even you—to hold certain biases about certain groups of people or some individuals without realizing it. Teachers and educators who want to establish safe learning environments and practice culturally responsive teaching—thus giving all students an equal opportunity to achieve success—must recognize this. The biases that teachers have can affect the way they treat different students. It can also affect the expectations that they have of them. For instance, they might expect girls to not do as well as boys in math and science classes. The problem with this is that the way teachers and educators behave toward students and the expectations they place on them influences the way those children behave. Let us say that a little girl got a really good grade in math class and did better than most of her classmates, including all the boys. Her teacher said, "I cannot believe this. Girls aren't really good at math," before that girl and the whole class. Throughout the year, this teacher made remarks such as, "It is ok if you cannot get it, I didn't really expect you to anyways," to the girls. This kind of reaction is bound to influence girls' subconscious thought patterns in class. This will in turn affect their motivation, attitude, and behavior. As a result, girls will be more likely to underperform in math class from then on. This will of course include the girl that had initially gotten really good grades. This is just a small example of how teachers' and educators' implicit biases and expectations can influence student behavior and academic performance. Considering this, it is vital that teachers periodically assess themselves and their behavior to see what implicit biases and expectations they hold. In doing so, they can identify the biases they hold and begin correcting their behavior as needed.

Assess Your Behavior

So, how precisely can teachers and educators identify their implicit biases? How can they go about assessing their behavior? There are several ways in which they can do this. The first is taking what's called an Implicit Association Test or IAT (National Association of Multicultural Education, 2014). Tonya R. Moon, the Chair of the Institutional Review Board for the Social and Behavioral Sciences, created this test to help people identify the biases, preconceived ideas, and prejudices they hold, whether they are aware of them or not. The test can be taken by anyone, but it is especially important for teachers, who play such a significant role in shaping young lives, to take it. This research-based test concretely shows what implicit biases teachers may hold and how comfortable they really are when interacting with people of different races. Once teachers and educators take this test, they should be prepared to ask themselves certain questions. Were they surprised by the results, for instance? How do they think this newfound understanding can better equip them for engaging with students of diverse backgrounds and their parents and guardians? They should also think back to their past interactions and behaviors. Can they identify any instances where their implicit biases have clearly impacted the way they behaved? Are there any patterns that they can observe? Once teachers and educators answer these questions and do a thorough examination of their attitudes, they can then move on to correcting them. But more on that a little bit later.

Another tool teachers and educators can use to identify their implicit biases and how they affect their classroom is the Anti-Bias Classroom Observation Checklist Environmental Evaluation (Western Oregon University, 2010). This evaluation is made up of various questions teachers can ask themselves. If the answer to one question is "yes", they check the "yes" column. If it is "no", they check the "no" column. The checklist asks questions about the images portrayed in the classroom, the books the teacher uses, the in-class toys and equipment, and staff interactions. When evaluating classroom images, the checklist might ask a question like, "Do the images around the classroom appear to represent all children, families, and staff in the program?" When assessing the books in class, it may ask questions like, "Do the children's books depict a variety of family structures and income levels?" Finally, in assessing staff interactions, it may ask questions like, "Do the teachers/caregivers use visual aids, gestures, and physical prompts with children with cognitive disabilities or limited language skills?" Once teachers and educators have gone through the entire checklist, they can evaluate their scoreboard. How many questions have they answered with "yes"? How many have they answered with "no"? Based on this, they can move on to the reflection portion of the checklist. Here, they can consider whether the results showed that they and their classroom were biased or unbiased. They question whether they uncovered any biases they did not realize they had as they moved through the checklist. Then they can start listing suggestions for changing their behavior and the very environment that reigns in their classrooms.

Correct Behaviors

Once teachers have evaluated their behaviors and identified their hidden biases, the question becomes or should become, "How do I change my behavior?" There are several things that teachers and educators can do to change. The first is to make themselves aware of their biases. Taking the IAT or doing the checklist is the first step toward this. The next is to write down all the biases they have for each and every student. This will help them to remain aware of their biases and modify their behavior accordingly. Let us say that a student with ADHD is "acting up" and a teacher has recently realized that she has come to think of him as a troublemaker. In writing down this bias, she can actively remind herself of it. So, the next time this particular student "acts out," she will be able to remain calmer and handle the situation better and in a more thoughtful way. For instance, rather than tell the student to quiet down, she can try to refocus his attention by asking him what he thinks of the subject she is teaching. A similar kind of thing can be done with parents and guardians. A lot of teachers and instructors develop certain kinds of biases about students based on their socio-economic status, how fluent they are in English, and more. Becoming aware of this situation will help teachers and educators to refrain from projecting the biases or opinions they have of parents and guardians onto their kids (Classtime Blog, 2017). One fascinating way teachers can begin to break down their implicit biases about parents and guardians is by doing home visits (Faber, 2017). This is something that the Saint Paul Federation of Teachers and educators discovered for themselves when they began the Parent/Teacher Home Visit initiative. About 75% of teachers who did home visits have stated that the visits helped dismantle the beliefs they held about students' families. 93% of them meanwhile have said that the visits helped them get to know their students better. This is something that can only help break down further biases and allow teachers and educators to better understand how best they can help their students excel.

Another way teachers and educators can challenge their biases and change their behavior is by setting more expectations and standards for the entire class. You can then uphold each and every student in class to that very same standard. They all are bursting with the exact same kind of potential after all. Teachers and educators can also try grading students without looking at their names and thus knowing who they are. The way technology works these days more than allows for this. Evaluating an essay or an exam without knowing who worked on it is a great way of evaluating students accurately and without bias. This is something that the Boston Symphony itself discovered in 1952. At the time, the Boston Symphony was trying to find a way to increase the number of women in the orchestra. To make sure that no one fell victim to implicit bias, the symphony decided to hold blind auditions. Musicians performed behind stage curtains, and they even removed their shoes before coming on stage, so that whether they were wearing heels or not, they would not give their gender away. The end result was that 50% of the musicians chosen for the symphony were female. Until then, the Boston Symphony was mostly male (Weinstock, 2016). What this goes to show is that implicit bias can severely impact the way people behave. Teachers and educators are no exception to this rule. In becoming aware of their biases, however, they work to change their behavior and create massive change within their classrooms. The effectiveness of this change, however, is contingent on continuous monitoring. Biases can come back. They can change shape or form and insinuate themselves in people's lives in different, unique ways. People may become complacent and resort to old patterns of thought and behavior without meaning to. But if teachers are constantly vigilant, if they make sure to pull out their checklists regularly, they can avoid this pitfall. In doing so, they can ensure that they help each and every student in their class to thrive and give them the equal opportunities they deserve.

Chapter 4:

Benefits of Culturally

Responsive Teaching

Culturally responsive teaching was invented by an American teacher educator and pedagogical theorist called Gloria Ladson-Billingstan. Gloria's aim in coming up with this concept at the turn of the century was to find a better way to explore the academic potential of students that might have gone otherwise undiscovered (Saluja, 2021). Given her line of work, she probably knew better than anyone how often this happened. In devising her methodology, she tried to find ways of integrating students' cultural references into the classroom and lessons. Her methodology has since been picked up by other researchers such as Sonia Nieto and Geneva Gay, who recognized its value. These researchers saw the myriad of ways culturally responsive teaching can help students, teachers and educators, and parents and guardians. They recognized that education was essentially a catalyst for better job options and higher pay for students in the future. Hence, they have devoted their careers to expanding on it and making it a greater part of the current education system.

Benefits for Teachers and Educators

Culturally responsive teaching allows students to connect more with the subjects that they are being taught and thus do better in their classes. When students' engagement level in class increases, their grades, and academic performance improves. This reflects well on teachers, whose performance and success in their chosen careers are directly tied to the performance and success of their students. After all, if a teacher's students consistently do poorly in their class, then does the fault really lie with the students or with that teacher's methodology? Most people would conclude that the fault is with the teacher. In that case, why would any school hire that specific teacher or keep them on their staff?

Culturally responsive teaching methods help teachers and educators get their students interested in the subjects they are teaching. When students get interested, they get more engaged in class. This means that they participate in class discussions more, become less likely to skip classes, actually learn in class, and do their homework well and thoroughly. Observing students as they work and study to the best of their abilities, teachers gain valuable insights about them. For instance, they start being able to identify the specific strengths and weaknesses of certain students. If, for example, they notice that one student has trouble concentrating and sitting still for more than 25 minutes, this is something that they can make note of. They can then use this information to tailor certain in-class assignments and the homework that they devise to cater to that child's needs. In doing so, they can give him the solid base he needs to perform well in class. Culturally responsive teaching, then, makes it possible for teachers and educators to develop their unique methods of engagement in class, thus ensuring that they capture all students' attention and interest. It also makes it easier for them to meet the needs of different kinds of students.

When teachers and educators understand students' different needs, they become able to respond to them. When they respond to their students' needs in full, they start expanding their own horizons. Contrary to what some might think, students aren't the only ones who can learn new things in classrooms and in school settings. Teachers and educators and educators can learn a thing or two as well. For instance, they can learn and begin to appreciate different perspectives that they otherwise would never have become familiar with. In doing so, they can start seeing the unique qualities and strengths of individuals from different cultures and backgrounds. This newfound understanding can help them to expand their way of thinking and develop their emphatic capabilities. Put simply, culturally responsive teaching can stimulate the emotional and cognitive growth of teachers and educators as individual human beings.

This situation will typically foster what's known as social-emotional learning in classrooms. Social-emotional learning (SEL) is an educational method that, true to its name, fosters emotional and social skills in class (Casel, 2022). It, for instance, actively helps students strengthen their emphatic capabilities. Like culturally responsive teaching, SEL tends to positively impact students' academic performance. At the same time, it helps improve classroom behavior, thus reducing class disruptions. This leads to a calmer, easier-to-manage class environment populated by mostly well-behaved students, something that every teacher wants. This kind of environment lowers everyone's stress levels—including the teachers'—and can even lower depression levels among students and educators.

That culturally responsive teaching supports SEL means that teachers and educators who adopt this methodology are able to create a more welcoming environment for all students, regardless of what kind of background or culture they come from. This kind of environment prioritizes inclusion, rather than exclusion, ensuring that no one is left behind in any way. Teachers and educators and students are able to develop authentic, trusting, and caring relationships in class, which allows teachers and educators to adequately support their students when the need arises. This environment also helps students develop better, more caring relationships with one another, which effectively reduces in-class conflicts. This, again, makes for a much calmer, easier-to-manage teaching environment for teachers and educators. It, therefore, enables them to do the best job they possibly can.

Benefits for Parents

As we've already seen, culturally responsive teaching has certain benefits for parents and guardians as well. For one, it makes them feel more welcome on school grounds and actively invites them to participate in their children's learning experiences and academic lives. Parents thus become less hesitant about participating in school-related activities such as volunteer opportunities and PTA meetings. This positively impacts their children's overall behavior, making them less likely to do things like skipping school. Students whose parents and guardians participate in their school lives generally do better academically, which is something that all parents and guardians want for their children.

The reason parent participation in school impacts students so much is that parents and guardians who feel respected and welcome at school develop a specific attitude toward education. This attitude is then picked up by their children, whether they realize it or not. If parents and guardians adopt a positive attitude towards education and learning, their children will notice, observe, and embrace this attitude. If parents and guardians show through their behavior that school and learning are top priorities, then their children will begin to make them priorities as well. Continually attending PTA meetings and parent-teacher conferences, for instance, certainly would signal to students that their parents and guardians are making their education a priority. Having received this message, these students will be far more likely to make their own education a priority too.

Another critical benefit culturally responsive teaching has for parents and guardians is that it enables them to support their children during their academic lives a great deal more than they otherwise would have been able to. Let us say that there is a boy who has been having difficulty in math class. This boy's mother goes to a parent-teacher conference and his teacher relays this problem to the mother. The teacher, having observed in class that the boy has concentration problems, tells the mother that this is why her son is having trouble. Perhaps the teacher even tells the mother that she suspects her son might have attention deficit and hyperactivity disorder (ADHD). The mother, having learned this, then goes home and has a talk with her. Rather than berate her son about his poor performance in class, as she might have done had the teacher not shared her concerns, she discusses the boy's concentration issues with him. After their talk, she has her son start meditating regularly to improve his focus.

Maybe she even has him evaluated by a professional and gets a diagnosis for him. Having received a diagnosis, she has her son meet regularly with a therapist to work on his concentration issues. Maybe she even gets him a prescription, if it turns out that his ADHD is severe enough. Whatever course of action this mother adopts, the point is that she becomes able to offer her son the support she needs, because she gets a full understanding of what his struggles and needs are. If this mother had not gone to meet with her son's teacher, however, she might not have ever realized that her son's poor academic performance was linked to his undiagnosed ADHD. Because she never realized this, she would have been far more likely to be disappointed in or angry at her son, which would not have helped him to overcome the hurdle standing before him. In fact, it likely would have disheartened him further, making him perform even worse in his math class.

One additional benefit of culturally responsive teaching is that it improves communication between parents and guardians and their children. In the ADHD example, for instance, the mother and son openly communicate about the son's concentration issues. This open and judgment-free communication allows the mother to help her son. The son, in turn, feels that he has heard, seen, and supported, which makes him grow closer to his mother. It also makes it more likely that he will come to her for her guidance and help should he face other kinds of issues in the near or far future, be they academic in nature or not. Similarly, culturally responsive teaching also improves communication between parents and guardians, and teachers. Let us go back to the ADHD example once more. If the teacher in this scenario had not discussed her observations and thoughts with the mother openly and honestly, the mother perhaps would not have had any idea what her son was going through. By communicating these things to the mother, the teacher effectively gave her the information and tools she needed to help her son. In doing so, she increased the trust that this mother had in her as her son's educator. Trust between parents and guardians and teachers and educators is vital within the education system. The two parties need to work together, after all, to support the kids within the education system in both school and home settings. The only way this can be done is if they openly communicate with one another and support each other by sharing any and all relevant information about the children they are trying to help succeed.

Another benefit of culturally responsive teaching is that by making parents and guardians an active part of their children's academic lives, they give them the opportunity to be true role models for their children. Children need role models in their lives to literally model their behavior, attitude, and ways of thinking after. Parents who participated in school would model school participation to their children. These children would therefore be more likely to participate more in their own academic lives by taking their own mothers, fathers, or guardians as their role models. Of course, parents and guardians who want to be good role models for their kids do not do so just by displaying a specific kind of attitude towards school and the education system as a whole. They also do so by adopting the types of behaviors that they want their children to adopt and emulate. In doing so, they create a kind of learning environment at home that supports their children's academic journeys and accomplishments. One thing parents and guardians can do to support building this kind of home learning environment is to read at home. By modeling this behavior, they can set an example for their kids and make it more likely that they will pick up the habit. They can also encourage their kids to read books themselves, once they are all enough to read. Similarly, they can offer praise and encouragement for good behaviors that will support their learning experience both in and outside of the home. When offering praise though, it would be better to praise and acknowledge children's efforts rather than the results that they achieve. If a child has gotten a good grade in their history exam, for instance, praising the effort she put into studying or that exam rather than the exam result would be a good idea. This will give her the message that what matters is her hard work and effort—

something that she can control and will more often than not lead to good results anyways.

Benefits for Students

We've already seen that culturally responsive teaching has numerous benefits for students. To quickly recap, these benefits are as follows:

- They make students more interested in the subjects that they are learning.

- They improve students' academic performance.

- They make students feel that they belong in the learning environment that is created in class and at school.

- They increase the trust students have in their teachers.

- They ensure that students' struggles, weaknesses, and problems are understood by the responsible adults around them and therefore ensure that their needs are actually met.

- They decrease the stress, anxiety, and depression levels that students might be feeling.

- They improve the relationship between students and their classmates or schoolmates, creating greater understanding between them, regardless of what kinds of backgrounds and cultures they come from.

All that being said, the benefits of culturally responsive teaching methods actually extend beyond the classroom and students' academic lives. In other words, culturally responsive teaching has long-term benefits for students. One of these benefits is that it ensures they remain in the education system for a long time—till they graduate from high school at the very least. It makes them more likely to go to some kind of university and college post-graduation. This is beneficial for students because the more education they get, the better their prospects for future employment and earnings will be. According to one study, the unemployment rate for individuals who pursued their doctoral degrees was 1.7% and their median weekly earnings were around 1,623$. By comparison, the unemployment rate for individuals who acquired their bachelor's degree was 2.3% and their median weekly earnings were around 1,137$. The employment rate of those individuals who did not have high school diplomas, on the other hand, was 8% and their median weekly earnings were around 493$ (Vilorio, 2016). The discrepancy here is obvious to see. Of course, education alone does not guarantee that a person will be able to find employment. It does, however, improve students' chances of finding employment and being paid well. This is why keeping students in school by using the suitable education methodologies, such as culturally responsive teaching, is so important.

The link between education level and the employment rate is not the only reason why culturally responsive teaching should be adopted by the education system to a greater extent. Another is the very clear connection between education and health. The more educated someone is, the more access they will have to better health. An educated person, like someone who has a bachelor's degree, usually has more income or access to greater resources and reaps greater psychological or social benefits—for instance, it reduces their stress levels and thus prevents these levels from damaging their health—and lives in more affluent, healthier neighborhoods (Virginia Commonwealth University, 2015). All of these things give them access to better and greater health resources, which in turn ensures that they live a healthier life.

Beyond that, educated people tend to exhibit healthier behaviors. For example, they tend to have healthier diets or exercise regularly. This is because they know what they need to do to maintain their health, as well as the consequences of not doing those things. Some doctors have observed that educated patients are more likely to follow whatever instructions they have been given, advocate for themselves when they need to, understand their health needs more thoroughly and properly, and communicate better and more openly with their healthcare providers.

If culturally responsive teaching makes students more likely to keep pursuing their education—and it does— then that means that it makes them better job opportunities and higher-paying positions. It also means that they will be better able to take care of their health and lead healthier lifestyles. Luckily, more and more people have become aware of this fact, even if the education system has not fully embraced culturally responsive teaching yet. This is why overall student dropout rates have been decreasing over the past years.

In 2010, for instance, the overall student dropout rate in the United States was 7.4%. In 2020, this rate dropped down to 5.3% (National Center for Education Statistics, 2020). Looking at these rates a little more closely, it is easy to see the role culturally responsive teaching has played in this situation. Between 2010 and 2020, the student dropout rate among Hispanic students dropped down from 15.1% to 7.4%, after all. Similarly, the student dropout rate among Black students has dropped down from 8% to 4.2% in the same time period. It is highly debatable whether this would have been the case had it not been for the rise of culturally responsive teaching in a variety of schools and educational institutions.

Chapter 5:

Methods of Culturally

Responsive Teaching

Now that we know all the short-term and long-term benefits of culturally responsive teaching, let us take a closer look at its methodologies and practices. How do you go about adopting culturally responsive teaching? Where do you begin? What methods and techniques can you make use of? What do you need to implement these methods and techniques? Once you've adopted culturally responsive teaching, how can you start evaluating your performance? How can you measure if it has had any impact on your students?

There are several methods of culturally responsive teaching. As a teacher, it is your job to examine these methods and find the ones that work best for you and them. The method you choose must embody the elements of culturally responsive teaching. These elements might sometimes slip your mind. You are only human, after all. Luckily, there is a handy checklist you can use to ensure that this does not happen (Howard, 2020):

- Culturally responsive teaching must nurture your students' academic skills, as well as their psychological, emotional, social, physical, and, of course, cultural well-being.

- It must recognize that your classroom is made up of individuals that come from very varied cultural and socio-economic backgrounds.

- It must therefore take care to adopt dynamic teaching practices that recognize all these cultures and differences and incorporate them into the curriculum.

- Culturally responsive teaching must involve parents and guardians and even their communities in their children's academic lives and learning experiences.

- It must ensure that the subject matters that are being taught are placed within students' own cultural contexts, thus allowing them to connect with their classes.

Once you've chosen and are implementing your culturally responsive teaching methods, make sure that they embody and adhere to these essential elements. Keep this checklist on hand as you explore the myriad of methods of culturally responsive teaching out there that you can choose from.

The Methods

There is a staggering multitude of culturally responsive teaching methods you can choose from as you devise your curriculum for the year. You can select a number of these methods to create the kind of learning environment you want and find the ones that work best for you. The first method you can try is to activate your students' prior knowledge. This method involves asking students what they already know about the subject you are about to cover in class. By doing this, you'll be able to make them active participants in the lesson, rather than passive listeners. You'll also be able to ensure that they connect more with what you are about to teach them and build on what they already know. You can pair this technique with another, which is to interview students. By interviewing students, you can understand their values and habits, especially learning habits. Individual interviews with students will let you get to know each of them well and form a personal connection with them, which is very important in culturally responsive teaching. When you are interviewing students, you can inquire what their hobbies and interests are. You can also ask what their favorite subjects, lessons, and assignments are. You can then use all this knowledge to craft teaching methods and assignments that cater to how they learn. For instance, once you've discovered what their interests are, you can make them part of the class. In doing so, you'll be able to get your students more interested in what you are teaching them. Let us say you are teaching math class for instance. Math is a subject that many students find boring. One of your students—a boy called Matt—indeed finds it boring. Matt, however, is very interested in soccer. If you ask him to solve a regular math problem, he might be less engaged in class. But if you give him a math problem where he has to calculate the speed with which Ronaldo has to kick a ball in order to score a goal and win the championship game? Well, Matt might be a little more interested in math in this case. The same kind of thing can be done with a multitude of things, not just interests and hobbies. Students' cultures, customs, traditions, and habits can easily be incorporated into a variety of different classes. This would make lessons both more interesting for them and far more memorable.

All of this can go part and parcel with another teaching method which is to contextualize learning. Let us say you are a history teacher. The subjects that you are teaching will obviously pertain to different time periods, geographies, and cultures. As such, some students may find it hard to connect to them. You can, however, overcome this issue by making an effort to connect the lessons to the times you live in. If you are studying

American history, for instance, asking your students what George Washington would think about American society today might be a very interesting and engaging exercise. You can take this technique a step further too by integrating current world problems and events into your class. If a new law has been passed, for instance, having your students discuss how George Washington—or other historical characters—would have responded to it might be one course to follow. Having them come up with arguments for and against this law, as George Washington would if he were for or against it would be another.

Linking the subjects you are discussing in class to current events and modern times when you can, can allow you to employ another effective method: openly discussing and debating social and political issues. By hosting such discussions, you'll give your students a safe space where they can share their opinions and encounter different perspectives they otherwise would not have considered or come across. Let us say you are reading Mary Wollstonecraft's *Vindication of the Rights of Women*, in class. Hold a class discussion where you can hear about how students of different cultural backgrounds and different genders react to the ideas that Wollstonecraft presented in her book. How do different people respond to these ideas? What new perspectives do they bring to the table? Doing so can help you to create very memorable, impactful discussions in class while allowing your students to connect to the book you are discussing on a much deeper level. Another thing that can help with this is to have students whose native languages aren't English contribute to the class using their own languages. Language is a unique thing, in that some words that exist in one language do not exist in others. A student who speaks a foreign language, then, might spot some idea in the subject matter that you are discussing whose essence is encapsulated in a word or saying in his own language. Letting that student share his language with the class in this case, then, could help students grasp that concept better. It can also allow that student to form a connection to and understanding of a work that he otherwise might have missed out on.

Of course, the use of new vocabulary is not just limited to foreign languages. Using new terminology pertaining to different interests and hobbies to explain otherwise complicated concepts and theorems could be a great way of engaging students in class. This could make classes more understandable for them. Using a basketball analogy, for instance, when you are describing an art movement can help you to overcome certain barriers to learning. So can incorporating popular culture into your class. Say, you are discussing the works of Shakespeare in English class. Shakespeare can be notoriously difficult to get through. But what if you were to liken the author's poetic language to rap? What if you were to discuss *Romeo and Juliet* as though it were a soap opera or a really dramatic Netflix show? What if you were to have your students act out scenes from *Macbeth* or *Hamlet* and thus put on sketches for the class? Such things can make lessons a lot more fun for students. They can also make hard-to-grasp subjects easy to understand.

One technique you can use to get students more involved in class is to invite guest speakers of different backgrounds and cultures. Let us say you are discussing World War II in class. Having a war veteran come to class and give an account of some of his experiences could be fascinating for your students. It can get them to think deeper about what they are learning and explore novel avenues of thought. Having a climate expert come in and discuss the future of the world—without painting too bleak a picture—for science class could do the same thing. Ensuring that guest speakers are of diverse cultures and backgrounds would be essential for this technique to work best though. Studies show, after all, that students tend to work harder when they come from similar backgrounds as their educators or lecturers (Egalite et al., 2015). Keep this in mind when you are choosing guest speakers to invite to your class.

A lot of teachers and educators think that learning can only happen in traditional lecture scenarios. This, however, is not the case. It is especially untrue in the case of very young students, who tend to be very energetic and who typically have short attention spans. Students learn best when different learning methods are taken into account. Some students do learn best in traditional lecture settings. Others do not. Given that, it would be best to rotate between different teaching tools and methods such as solving puzzles, playing games, having in-class trivia competitions, doing experiments, watching videos, reading articles, creating artwork, and, of course, giving lectures. By using a full roster of teaching tools in class, you can make sure that you are addressing every student's learning needs.

Games and playing are often underestimated in schools and classrooms. That play and gamifying subjects make things fun creates the impression that they are not serious methods of teaching. However, playing games is an incredibly effective teaching tool. Gamifying lesson elements can therefore be a great thing to try out in your classroom. Testing students' knowledge by dividing them into groups and holding trivia competitions between them could be one way of gamifying the class. This would be very effective in social studies, science, and English classes, for example. Other forms of gamifying lessons might be offering rewards or badges for completing certain goals and assignments and creating instruction booklets for classes that outline the best way to earn high grades in specific classes. You can also set learning goals for the class—rather than for individual students—and chart class progress throughout the week, month, or semester. This could be incredibly motivating for students.

Some students might be hesitant to participate in class. Some may be shy or introverted. Others may be struggling with a language barrier. Calling on each student, without showing favoritism or preference for some, is an excellent culturally responsive teaching method to use in these cases. This technique gives everyone an equal opportunity to speak and share their thoughts. It allows students the platform they need to voice what they are thinking. There may be some students in your class who have valuable contributions to make but are unable to make them because they are hesitant to speak. Calling on them would subvert this issue. Providing them with the opportunity to speak would encourage them to participate in class more and boost their confidence. Of course, this technique will work a lot better if you take care to know each student in your class. Learn your students' names, so that you'll know them when you ask them a question. Know their likes, interests, and dislikes. In doing so, you can increase the trust between the two of you and make them feel that they are valued members of the community you create in class—something that is absolutely necessary if you want to establish a safe learning space for all.

Using different kinds of materials, such as sound clips, videos, and images is very important in class. Such supplementary materials take into account different learning styles and make classes more memorable for students. However, you must use supplementary materials that represent a wide range of cultures, ethnicities, backgrounds, and family structures. Where visual materials are concerned, this might mean including videos and images of people of different ethnicities. Where audial materials are concerned, it might mean including clips in different languages or even accents. The fact is students process lessons a lot quicker if different cultures and languages are incorporated into those lessons or so studies suggest (Howard, 2016).

One method you can try to increase student participation in class might be to ask your students to propose ideas for projects and other big assignments. This can boost their confidence and creativity and allow them to showcase their various strengths. If something that a student proposes does not quite meet the criteria you've set out for them, have them work on it more, rather than dismissing the idea. How can they improve their project proposal? What can they do to improve upon their idea? Have a list of project ideas on hand in case a student has trouble coming up with one. That way, you can present the list to that student, and they can choose the one that appeals most to them. Because the student retains their right of choice in this scenario, they will be more interested and engaged in the project than they otherwise might have been.

Explore different learning methods during free time and study periods. During study periods you can offer your students a variety of learning tools to choose from. In doing so, you'll be giving them the opportunity to work with things that suit their learning methods best. If you offer students audiobooks as well as physical books, for instance, those who learn better by listening can choose audiobooks. If you have educational games and experiments on hand, then those students who learn best by doing will be able to advance much quicker in class. Allowing students who work best in teams to collaborate on some assignments and projects, while permitting others to work solo if that option suits them best would also be a good idea.

There is such a thing as learning by teaching. This is where one student teaches a subject they are good at to another student. This is something that helps both students. The student teaching the "lesson" for instance, gets to practice and reinforce what they know. The student who is listening gets to learn and practice a concept they are struggling with by working together with their peers. Hosting activities such as reading a passage and discussing it as a group or working in pairs to finish an experiment are equally effective learning tools. This is because, like the tutoring example, it allows students to collaborate and support one another. It reinforces teamwork and ensures that students can fill each other's gaps in knowledge if they exist. This gives everyone the same learning opportunity and allows them to excel.

Another method of doing this is establishing what's known as cooperative base groups (Guido, 2017). Collaborative base groups are composed of three or four students each. The groups work together throughout the semester and meet regularly as they try to reach the learning goals that are set for their groups. Because these goals are set for all of them, rather than each of them as individuals, they end up having to support one another's learning, fill in gaps and correct any misunderstandings. Once you've divided students into their groups, help them to set up regular meeting times. During these meeting times, students can review the things they have learned that week or month, answer each other's questions, and complete assignments together. Forming a cooperative base group is a very effective culturally responsive teaching method because it allows students to express what they learn in their own terminology and language. In other words, it enables them to contextualize what they have learned in their own language and share it with others.

Finally, considering how important parent involvement is for students' academic success, writing take-home letters for parents and guardians can be a great culturally responsive teaching tool as well. It can provide parents and guardians with a firm understanding of what their children are learning and how they are doing in class. Thanks to this, parents and guardians can help with their children's homework, for instance, a great deal more. They can also keep track of their children's progress, understand the struggles they are facing, and step in to support them when they need it.

Understanding What Is Needed

As you can see, there are a staggering number of culturally responsive teaching methods and techniques to choose from. All of them have one major commonality: understanding what students need and responding to it fully. This is why culturally responsive teaching methods prove so beneficial for students. When students' different needs are met, they become able to tackle the obstacles that might otherwise stand in their way. They become able to overcome language barriers, for instance, when they are provided with the language support they need, enabling them to fully understand what they are being taught in class (School of Education Blog, 2019). They give students the tools they need to overcome systemic barriers that, sadly, still exist in our education system. They solve representation issues, allowing students to see themselves more in the lessons they are being taught, thus increasing their interest in and engagement with them. To achieve this, teachers need to adopt seven key principles (Kentucky Department of Education, 2019):

1. They must set the same, high yet realistic, that is to say achievable, standards for all their students, regardless of their backgrounds.

2. They must be culturally sensitive. This means that they must make a conscious effort to get to know and understand their students, their families, and their circumstances.

3. In keeping with that, they must form positive relationships with their students' families and community and take steps to involve them in their children's academic lives as much as possible.

4. They must give students control of the lesson and the things they are learning from time to time, such as by allowing them to decide what project they want to work on. They must recognize that in doing so they boost their student's confidence and creativity while having them reinforce what they have learned.

5. Teachers and educators must use active, rather than passive learning methods. While lectures

will have to be given from time to time, classes should not be composed solely of instructive lectures and must include a variety of teaching methods and activities that increase class participation.

6. Teachers and educators should position themselves as a facilitator of knowledge, rather than adopting the typical hierarchical structure found in traditional teaching methods.

7. Teachers and educators should have students working in pairs and groups from time to time so that students can support each other's learning, reinforce the things they have learned and strengthen their bonds with their classmates.

The effectiveness of culturally responsive teaching can easily be observed in class throughout a semester or year. However, one other excellent way of gauging this is by having students write student evaluations. These evaluations can be of you, as a teacher, of the class you are teaching, and of themselves as students. In evaluating their teachers and class, students can clearly lay out what works for them and what would work better for them. In other words, students can share how their needs are being made and how they can be further met. They can also evaluate their performance, how they have improved over the semester and year and what they can still work on. In doing so, they can familiarize themselves with their strengths and weaknesses. By sharing these with you, they will give you what you need to further tailor your classes to fit their play to their strengths and address their weaknesses. Finally, by writing such evaluations, students can become an even greater part of their own learning experience and thus more invested in their academic performance and journeys.

Chapter 6:

Ongoing Responsibilities

Teachers and educators have an enormous responsibility on their shoulders: educating the future. It is their responsibility to ensure that their students learn what they need to become successful adults building successful lives for themselves. It is likewise their responsibility to support them on their academic journey, especially when they face struggles or hurdles. Teachers and educators who want to meet this responsibility in full, however, need to understand that not every child comes from ideal family situations and home environments. Studies show that a majority of children experience some kind of trauma before they reach adulthood (Orane, 2022, p. 160). Now, trauma can mean a lot of different things. Being bullied would certainly count as childhood trauma, for instance, So might having parents and guardians going through a messy divorce. The worst kinds of trauma, though, are those that involve abuse, neglect, and poverty. Such things can impact children's cognitive development, behavior, and academic performance significantly. Teachers and educators who want to help support all their students equally must be aware of this fact. They must make an effort to understand what kind of background their students come from, and what types of difficulties they have potentially experienced to tailor their education methods and interaction styles and approach those students accordingly.

Difficult Home Situations

Not every child comes from the same kind of home situation. Different children come from a variety of different home settings, family arrangements, and socioeconomic conditions. As such, it is essential to keep in mind that not every home environment is the same. In fact, some home situations are very stressful, even traumatic for children. Poverty is a significant cause of trauma for children and teens. Poverty typically equals a lack of resources, which can make doing schoolwork or even concentrating on classes difficult. It can also translate to a lack of monitoring and supervision for kids. If a child's parents and guardians are working two jobs each to make ends meet, for instance, that child will have little to no parental supervision at home. This will render them vulnerable at home or in their neighborhood to potential predators. Situations like this can make children feel unsafe or maybe uncared for. It can be a great source of pressure, seeing as they will have to fend for themselves at home or even take care of their younger siblings while their parents and guardians are away. At the same time, they will have to do their schoolwork or prepare for exams and such things will add to the stress they are already under.

The kind of things that children have to deal with in their home situations, then, can become sources of trauma for them. The trauma that children experience is something that leaves a significant mark on their psyche. It is something that affects both their mood and their behavior. This is because trauma is something that reduces the brain activity of developing children (Orane, 2022, p. 160, chapter 4). This includes teens, seeing as children's brains keep developing well into and past adolescence. That said, trauma affects different individuals in different ways. A girl who has grown up in a neglectful environment, for instance, might turn out to be the kind of student who disliked talking in class. She might be on the quieter side. She might hesitate to participate in class discussions because she does not know what to do or what she is supposed to do. A boy who comes from a similar kind of neglectful environment, on the other hand, might turn out to be the exact opposite of this girl. This boy might turn out to be loud and disruptive, someone prone to be labeled as a "troublemaker". The trauma of neglect might drive this boy to try and draw whatever attention he can. He might keep misbehaving in class because he needs the attention he is not getting at home.

The different ways that trauma can impact student behavior is something teachers have to recognize if they want to help their students thrive and succeed. To be able to do that, they must recognize different patterns of behavior such as cries for help and signs of distress that they are. One behavior that is a pretty obvious cry for help is absenteeism. Absenteeism is skipping class or school. Absenteeism can be a sign of many different things, lack of parental monitoring or presence at home. It can also be a sign of parental neglect or even abuse. For instance, a student who has gotten a black eye at home might choose to skip for a couple of days, so that no one discovers what happened to them.

Like absenteeism, retention is a sign of distress as well. Retention means a student neglecting their grades or doing poorly in class. It often happens when students are unable to keep up with their coursework due to difficult home situations. If retention continues for long enough, it can demoralize students significantly, thus increasing their chance of dropping out of school.

Another noticeable sign of distress is behavioral problems. Things like disciplinary issues, aggression, and misbehavior in class are often cries for help, rather than deliberate attempts to derail classes. Aggression, for instance, is an expression of internalized anxiety and stress. It is how many children and teens cope with things such as abandonment issues, sadness, hopelessness, humiliation, and rejection. Behavioral problems such as this often negatively impact students' academic performance. This adds to the feelings of hopelessness, anger, or shame they may already be feeling, causing them to struggle even more at school. If the situation carries on for long enough, it can very easily cause children to drop out.

That things like behavioral problems, absenteeism, and retention are cries for help is something teachers and educators who want to help all of their students equally must absolutely keep in mind. A lot of teachers, particularly ones who abide by traditional teaching methods, consider these red flags to be signs of laziness, hostility, and aggression. As such, they choose to punish students who exhibit such behavior, rather than explore how they might help them. The problem with this is that it only aggravates students and therefore their behavior further. Sending a child to detention, for instance, does not help him to do better in class. Often, it contributes to him doing worse and adds to the compendium of negative feelings he is mired in. This only makes him keep acting out and soon a loop of poor academic performance or behavior and subsequent punishments are formed. This loop continues until the student stops trying and drops out or fails out of school.

Things do not have to be this way, though, as culturally responsive teachers well know. Teachers and educators can in fact help break this loop and truly help their students in the process. They just need to know how. The first step to breaking this loop is to recognize the cries for help that students are making. Solving a problem is only possible once we realize that there is a problem, after all. When done, teachers and educators can begin addressing the real, underlying issues at hand. To that end, the first thing they can do is get help from counselors and social workers. They can talk to the school counselor in confidence for instance and share their observations with them. They can then ask what the correct approach and response to give is. Should they give the student in question a little space to deal with how he is feeling following an incident or should they calmly pull them to the side later on and have a discussion with them? By talking to counselors or social workers, teachers can get expert guidance and help. Thus, they can learn how to best help their students on a case-by-case basis.

Another thing teachers can do to truly help their students is to provide a stable learning environment for them. Children who experience trauma are often shaken or impacted by sudden changes. They know from experience that change can be incredibly damaging to them. Because of this, they need an environment where they can feel safe and grounded. Teachers and educators can create such environments in their classes, thus easing these students' very active nervous systems. When a change has to be introduced to the class, teachers can preempt any possible issues by announcing and explaining that change in advance. For instance, if the seating plan is going to be changed in class, they can announce it a week in advance. They can describe how the new seating plan will be, thus giving their students enough time to prepare for it. They can adopt a similar approach where more minor changes are concerned. If a teacher's going to turn off the lights so they can watch a documentary in class, for instance, they can tell what they are about to do before they do it. Small measures like this can help teachers and educators to create very grounding, safe, and familiar environments for their students. It will therefore help students manage the stress they are feeling and enable them to do better in class.

Teachers and educators must also keep in mind that they should treat all their students with dignity both in the classroom and outside of it. Valuing students' dignity and self-esteem can help them to deal with a lot of negative feelings they might be struggling with. Children who experience trauma often feel humiliated or out of control. Hence, they act out in an attempt to feel in control or to overcome feelings of humiliation. Teachers and educators can help them feel better and feel that they matter simply by treating them with respect. They can help them to feel in control of their own lives and feelings by giving them a sense of safety, integrity, and stability in class. They can further augment this by giving them actual choices where they can. Having students choose their own essay topic for English class is an excellent example of this, for instance. So are allowing them to choose between taking a written or oral exam and whether they want to participate in the school play or not.

Adopting a positive attitude and taking care to inspire and encourage students, rather than punish and discourage them can be very effective in this regard as well. A positive approach can go a long way with students as it would impact how they feel about themselves, their class, and their teacher. Teachers and educators can extend this positive approach and support students' various interests or skills when they spot them. In doing so, they will be helping students develop healthy means of expressing their emotions.

They will also be empowering them through encouragement and positive reinforcement.

Finally, teachers and educators can support their students by showing them unconditional acceptance. That does not necessarily mean accepting students' behavior when they misbehave in class. But it can mean providing them with a safe space to go to where they can deal with their feelings when they are upset. Students could also take advantage of this safe space when they need a break. Allowing students to make use of such a space would help them to process difficult feelings when they arise without disrupting class. Once students have calmed down, they can rejoin class and concentrate on their lesson better.

Talk Therapy

Some students go through more difficult situations than others. As such, they sometimes need more help from their classmates. Recognizing when a student needs help is an essential part of being a culturally responsive teacher. So, how can teachers and educators support students when they see that they need help? The first thing that they can do is to try talk therapy. Talk therapy is a kind of treatment that addresses mental, emotional, and behavioral issues through discussion, active listening, and counseling. Teachers can use talk therapy methods when talking to their students and trying to help them. Encouraging students to talk about the things they are feeling, experiencing, and going through can be immensely helpful to students. A lot of times, students feel too ashamed or embarrassed to talk to people when they are going through something or have an issue. Let us say a student who is not able to have breakfast in the mornings because the family is going through some financial hardship. This student might feel embarrassed about this situation. So, rather than talk to a friend or teacher about it and ask for help, the student might keep quiet. This student might get antsy, aggressive, and irritated in class, seeing as this student will be going without food till lunchtime. The student's mood will also likely sour because his or her blood sugar will be very low as well. A teacher who notices the change in this student's behavior will have to choose between one of two options. Either the teacher can punish the student for disrupting class, or the teacher can talk to him or her in private later on and inquire about what's going on. The teacher can encourage the student to talk and assure that the student has nothing to feel embarrassed or ashamed about. By encouraging the student to talk, without pushing this student, the teacher can understand the real problem, and come up with a solution for it— the teacher can arrange for a sandwich to be given to this student every morning, before the first period, for instance—and help her student to deal with what this student is feeling and experiencing.

Knowing when and where to speak to students is critical to talk therapy. If the teacher in the above example tries to talk to her student in front of the class, their talk likely will not go very well. If, on the other hand, the teacher makes an effort to talk this student in private, the teacher will be able to help this student a great deal more. Some students find it easier to talk when they have something else to focus on. Considering this, a teacher who wants to have a talk with a student might ask for that student's help with something. If you have a student you'd like to talk to, try talking to them while they are working on a project you've asked them to help you out with. This strategy would make it easier for the student in question to share whatever is troubling to this student; being the person to begin the conversation would as well. If you are trying to encourage a student to talk, start the conversation yourself. Begin by voicing your own insecurities. If you think a student is dealing with a particular issue, relate your own relevant and, of course, age-appropriate experiences. This way you can show that everyone feels embarrassed or sad sometimes. You can show your students that they are not alone. This can make students relax a little bit and make it more likely that they will open up to you.

Another interesting strategy that teachers can adopt to help get their students to open up to them when they need to is to use Cognitive Behavior Therapy or CBT. CBT is a therapy technique that focuses on the individual's—in this case the student's—experiences. It helps them to cope with feelings of fear, shame, pain, loss, and more. Learning Cognitive Behavioral Therapy methods or getting a certification in CBT can give teachers the tool they need to support and assist their students. CBT is all about reframing situations. With CBT, you can work toward reframing triggers to painful memories when students open up to you. You can help them to overcome those triggers by talking about how different the current situation is from the past. You can also further this along by reminding them that they are in a safe place populated with people who love and care for them.

Teachers and educators who have such conversations with students and understand their problems better can also help them to put coping strategies in place for when they are triggered. It should be remembered though that coping strategies do not mean suppressing emotions. That would be detrimental to students and likely worsen whatever behavioral problems they have been exhibiting. However, coping strategies can involve reminding students that they are capable of feeling more than one thing at a single time. They can feel upset about something and still remind themselves that they are in a safe place where they are loved and cared for. This reminder will help them to cope with whatever feeling is coursing through them at that moment.

One last thing teachers and educators wanting to help their students should bear in mind is that they should regularly check in with their students. Asking students how they are feeling and what you can do to help can get them to open up a great deal. It can stop students from bottling things up and reaching out for support when it is so plainly offered. It can also give students the message that they can come to their teachers when they are ready to talk and need help. This works best when coupled with positive reinforcement, wherein teachers and educators make sure to regularly provide their students with positive feedback whenever possible. This is because positive feedback strengthens the bond that teachers and educators are forming with students and increases the sense of safety, they have with them.

Incorporating Culture Into Class

One other responsibility that teachers take on when they step onto school grounds is ensuring students from different cultural backgrounds become interested and invested in their classes. They are responsible for making sure that these students feel they belong in the category and that they succeed academically. While this book has already covered the culturally responsive teaching techniques that ensure this, it has not yet touched on the strategies teachers and educators can adopt to internalize them. Teachers and educators need to be in the right, bias-free mentality in order to be able to internalize and implement culturally responsive teaching methods. This requires one crucial thing for them: knowing who they are as individuals. We all come from different cultural backgrounds. This includes teachers as well as students. The background that a teacher comes from can well influence how they teach their classes, interact with their students, and approach their subject matters (Truzy, 2017). It can also influence how they prefer conducting a class. Some teachers, for instance, find having children raise their hands in class too formal and thus do not implement it as a rule. Others absolutely require it. The culture that a teacher comes from can play a part in preferences and decisions like this. It can similarly affect what kinds of expectations teachers set for their students. As such, teachers should make a point of taking stock of themselves—their own backgrounds, values, and expectations—before ever setting foot in class. Only in doing so can they consciously begin altering their behavior, if they see that the need calls for it, and tend to their student's needs to the best of their ability.

In keeping with that, teachers and educators must recognize that every student learns in different ways. Some students learn better by taking notes. Others need to do experiments and learn by doing. Still, others might find watching documentaries or listening to audio clips the most effective form of learning. Being able to meet every student's needs means recognizing this fact. It means understanding that one style of learning might work for one student but not the other. Considering this, teachers and educators who want to help their students succeed must be flexible in their teaching methods. They must make sure that they incorporate different kinds of learning and teaching devices, methods, and tools into their daily curriculum. Only in doing so can they ensure they ensure they help all their students equally.

One of the most important things teachers can do for their students is to check biases at the door. This does not just extend to their own biases but their students' as well. The fact is teachers and educators are not the only ones who might have implicit biases. Students might suffer from such biases as well. This can cause a lot of trouble among students and interrupt the safe environment that has been created in class. Overcoming this situation is therefore vital for teachers and educators and the students they mean to support.

Chapter 7:

Getting All Students

Involved

Teachers and educators typically set the tone in a given classroom. The way they conduct their lessons and the way they interact with other students are things that students observe and pick up on. The attitude that a teacher displays in dealing with different kinds of students is something that students will emulate consciously or not. Because of this, it is a teacher's responsibility to lead by example in class. It is also a teacher's responsibility to introduce different cultures, perspectives, and backgrounds to students in class. The more knowledgeable a teacher is about other cultures, the better a job they will be able to do introducing those cultures to class. The more sensitive a teacher is to different perspectives and ways of thinking, the more sensitive their students will be too.

There is a myriad of ways teachers and educators can both showcase their sensitivity as examples to follow and expand their horizons and perspectives regarding other cultures. One thing teachers can try is to greet students in a different language every month. The ideal thing to do in this scenario would be to choose the same phrase to say every month, just in a different language (Cowling, 2017). For argument's sake, this phrase can be "Good morning!" Teachers and educators can start the semester off by saying good morning in English, then follow that up by saying "buenos dias" every day to their students for the following month. The month after that they can say the phrase in French, then Chinese, and so on. This simple practice can be a fun little exercise to make students more aware of the fact that there are different cultures and languages out there other than their own. It can help them to register that other people, including some of their classmates, speak these languages. Thus, it can evoke their curiosity about those languages and cultures. In doing so, teachers and instructors can begin the heavy task of making students realize that their different cultures have an array of commonalities.

Cultural Commonalities: Why Are They Important?

Establishing cultural commonalities requires forming an intercultural communication framework (ICF) in class (Decapua & Wintergerst, 2016, p. 31). An ICF is established in three steps. The first is forming and maintaining a relationship between students and teachers. To do this, teachers and students must truly understand each other's cultures, beliefs, and values. In sharing parts of their cultures with one another, they can learn from one another and create a mutual understanding that everyone can benefit from. When teachers and educators understand students' cultures, they gain a window of explanation as to why they might behave in certain ways. For instance, a teacher might see that a student is quiet in class not because that student is shy but because active participation is not a learning priority in her culture (Decapua & Wintergerst, 2016, p. 33). Having realized this, the teacher can properly grasp that student's discomfort at being called on in class. The teacher can then make certain accommodations to the teaching style, such as holding more small group activities in class so that the student does not feel singled out. She can reasonably adjust her teaching methods in light of what she has learned and observed about her students' culture.

Finding cultural commonalities is crucial because it makes this process a lot easier for both students and teachers. It can bridge gaps between students, teachers, and classmates. When students understand different elements of their classmates' cultures, they become more open-minded, tolerant, and accepting of them. This is because the unfamiliar becomes familiar to them. The environment within the classroom and the atmosphere among classmates are better as a result. Students grow closer to one another just as they grow closer to their teachers. This results in a decrease in problematic behaviors such as bullying. Negative perceptions, stereotypes, and behaviors such as bullying or ostracization falter in the face of cultural bridge building. Culturally responsive teaching allows students to find similarities between themselves while appreciating their differences.

Introducing different cultures might be a bit of a challenge for any teacher. Luckily, there are several easy-to-follow methods teachers and educators can use in this regard. A lot of these methods go hand in hand with social-emotional learning (SEL) as well, which makes finding cultural commonalities easier for students. Some examples of these methods are as follows:

1. Remain observant and present in the classroom. Watch how your students respond to their classmates of different cultures and backgrounds. Observe their interactions with each other and with you. In doing so, you can begin spotting commonalities and find ways of explaining differences, thus making them more understandable and easier to grasp.

2. Share stories of different people from different cultures during class. Incorporate such stories into class materials and have students discuss them. Stories have always been and always will be more appealing and memorable to human beings than facts. This is doubly true for students. Stories that they can see themselves in, and that they can emotionally connect with are powerful teaching tools. They can be used to introduce a wide variety of concepts to them, including different cultures. They can be used to draw out commonalities between various cultures and thus build bridges among students.

3. This former technique will be rendered infinitely more effective if it is followed up by class discussions. Discussing a story that was shared in class or something that students read as an assignment can get them to think about the learnings in those stories more. It can help students internalize the messages within those stories and expand their ways of thinking and behavior towards others.

4. Creating an atmosphere that is supportive of all is another critical component of all this. The thing is, not every discussion and conversation a teacher has in their classes will be easy. Some will be complex and difficult to navigate. Others will be triggering to some students for a variety of reasons. Ensuring that the classroom is a safe space in which these more challenging conversations can be had is crucial. Being an objective intermediary when potential conflict

arises within that space is equally vital. Only in doing so can teachers and educators give each student the sense of safety they need to learn to navigate thorny paths they may come up on, unwittingly or not.

5. One last thing a teacher can try to get students to understand their common cultural grounds better and respect their differences more is to give them short creative tasks or assignments in which they can showcase or implement what they learn. Having students write positive affirmations for one another could be one such assignment. Another might be challenging them to be more empathetic towards one another, even—and especially—in cases where their perspectives and thoughts on certain things differed. By doing this, teachers can help students develop their emphatic capabilities and support their growth as friends whose opinions sometimes differ from one another but who are able to respect each other nonetheless.

Chapter 8:

Software and Teaching

Aids

It should be clear by now that teachers and educators that want to adopt culturally responsive teaching methods have their work cut out for them. They have so many different things to consider and keep in mind that some might feel a little overwhelmed when trying to embrace this methodology. Luckily, there is a wide array of software and teaching aids that teachers can make use of on their journeys. From video games—of all things—to culturally responsive computer technologies and technologies that facilitate parent-teacher communication, there is a near-infinite variety of devices and software that teachers and educators can choose from in the modern age.

Video Games as a Resource for Diversity

Games have long been a significant part of the education system. Culturally responsive teachers and educators can use games and play to teach new concepts and put the things that students learn into action, thereby making them more memorable. Such teachers and educators recognize games as essential educational tools that they are. Video games are no exception to this. Contrary to what some might think, playing video games has an array of benefits for students. For instance, they can improve students' spatial skills, critical thinking abilities, and problem-solving skills. They can also teach different cultural narratives about societies and social systems to students while getting them to engage with those cultures that are represented in-game (Richard, 2017, p. 37). The games *Civilization* and the *Assassins' Creed* series are great examples of games that do both. *Civilization*, for instance, can teach students about hypothetical historical scenarios, thus getting them to consider history and geography from new angles. The *Assassins' Creed* series, on the other hand, can directly show how much more culturally and ethnically diverse history was than what some people may think and some textbooks may portray. They can also do a very thorough job of educating students on history itself. That there have been numerous articles published in recent years, describing how some students passed their history exams because they regularly played *Assassin's Creed* is a testament to this (Geek & Sundry, 2018).

All that said, it should be noted that video games aren't perfect. They come with their own set of challenges and difficulties. One such challenge is that most game developers are lacking in diversity. For instance, only

2.5% of game developers in the industry are African American and only 7.3% are Latinx (Richard, 2017, p.38). This can translate to an on-screen representation issue or a stereotyping issue on screen. As such, teachers who mean to use video games as learning tools should be careful of which games they use. Such teachers should also be aware that there is a digital divide where gaming is concerned. Not all students have ready access to gaming devices. Some may not have access to computers where they can play such games. Others might not have steady internet connections or electricity. Relying on video games as learning tools can be problematic on account of this, that is unless a concentrated effort is made by teachers, schools, the education system, and even the gaming industry to lower technological access barriers to gaming.

Culturally Responsive Gaming Technologies

Video games are not the only technological tools teachers can turn to. There are an array of interactive, open-source programs, software, and apps teachers and educators can use nowadays as helpful teaching tools. These programs must be open source so they are accessible to all students, regardless of their socio-economic situation. Such tools can make learning more interesting for students and help them advance quickly in their academic lives. Because there are so many different programs teachers can choose from, they should keep specific rules in mind when making their choices. First, teachers and educators must ensure that the software and technologies they are choosing offer realistic and diverse representation to the students that will be using them (Frederick et al., 2009, p. 12-13). If not, then students' engagement levels will go down as a result of their not being able to connect with the program they are given and the characters that populate it. Second, teachers must make sure that these teaching tools use the cultural and historical experiences of people of different backgrounds as a base to build. Programs that take care to do so build cultural competencies and thus get students more invested in what they are learning. Finally, teachers must ensure that the tools they choose give students the space they need to use their voices and express themselves freely. By doing so, they can have students tap into their creativity and innovation while increasing their interest in the program, as well as their self-confidence and self-esteem.

Take the program, the Hispanic Math Project as an example. This program was created by the Technology-Based Learning and Research Lab at Arizona State University. Its goal is to teach Latin, immigrant students time, money, geometric measurements, and other crucial things they will need to know. To do so, the Hispanic Math Project uses extraterrestrial characters in the game and features many culturally responsive design elements. For example, the characters in the game have extensive family structures, just as many Latinx people do. The system also gives users the option to choose between Spanish dialogues and directions and English ones. All of these steps and measures get students more interested in what they are being taught. As they spend more and more time on the platform, they absorb and internalize more and more information, without even realizing it (Frederick et al., 2009, p.10).

Another example of a culturally responsive technological teaching tool teachers could use is something called Rappin Reader. This program was created with African American boys in mind. It aims to use students' oratory skills to help them increase their literacy. At the same time, the program helps students improve their writing and critical thinking skills. The program achieves all this by having users create rap lyrics for their favorite artists. It uses their interest to help them advance their reading and writing skills and it gives them a creative and therefore fun way of doing so (Frederick et al., 2009, p.12). That the system thus allows for creative expression is a great bonus for most students.

Teacher and Parent Communication

Software and teaching aids can also be used to increase teacher and parent communication. Certain kinds of apps can help teachers and educators to overcome communication barriers between them and parents and guardians. For instance, if there is a communication barrier between parents and guardians and teachers, apps can be very helpful in solving it, especially if there is not an in-person interpreter to be of help. Apps like Class Tag and Bloomz, which were created by charter schools in Lee County, Florida, can be very helpful in this regard (de la Rosa, 2019).

Teachers and educators can use similar kinds of apps to send messages or pictures to send reminders of upcoming field trips, exam dates, and the like to parents and guardians. This way, they can easily keep parents and guardians in the loop and therefore engaged in their children's education. If English-language messages need to be sent to parents and guardians, then they can be done so with apps that have translation features. Apps with such features can be beneficial when the messages that need to be sent are more long-winded.

While using such technologies can be perfect for increasing parent participation in school, educators and schools need to make an active decision on how often they will use them to communicate with parents and guardians before the beginning of the school year (de la Rosa, 2019). If too many messages or updates are being sent to parents and guardians throughout the day or week, they might start checking the app much less frequently than they otherwise would. If parents and guardians are made to understand that any important messages and updates will be shared through these apps, however, they will be far more inclined to check it regularly and respond to incoming messages quickly. Establishing a well-developed communication plan is critical to this. This plan should include guidelines about how to use the chosen communication app. So is vetting the third-party vendors that devised the app to make sure that parents' guardians', and teachers' data will be kept safe.

Other Methods to Break Down Barriers

Language barriers aren't specific to the parents and guardians of students, as we've seen. In fact, they can be significant barriers for students as well. As such, the aforementioned app, software, and programs can be used to support bilingual children and non-native speakers in class as well. At the same time, teachers can adopt non-technological methods and devices they can keep using in class. In this way, they can lead a two-pronged assault on language barriers for students and enable them to overcome them.

The first supplementary method teachers can employ is to assign language buddies. This method, which was covered in the barriers to learning chapter, can help students who are non-native speakers to orient themselves better in class. It can enable them to follow along with the curriculum, understand the covered subjects, and do their assignments well. Also, the native and non-native students usually become good friends in these cases and support each other throughout the school year. This means that the language buddy system can be beneficial for all students, not just ones that struggle with English language classes.

Another method teachers can heavily rely on in their classes is to use visuals, as we've seen. Teachers who want to help their students overcome a multitude of barriers, not just ones pertaining to syllabi, can take this method a step further. They can do so by explaining classroom expectations, norms, and procedures using visuals as well. Hanging a large poster in class and walking students through such things can be very helpful in this regard. It can serve as an easy reminder for students, thus ensuring that they navigate their school lives much more smoothly than they otherwise might have. Labeling classroom objects bilingually—for instance in both English and Spanish—can be a way of building on this. Bilingual labeling can save students a great deal of embarrassment by mitigating the risk of their forgetting or mispronouncing a word. It also makes non-native speaker students more likely to talk and participate more in class. Think of it like this: Let's say a student isn't sure how to pronounce the word textbook or can't remember the word "textbook." He, therefore, doesn't know how to tell his teacher that he lost the textbook they were supposed to bring to class. The idea of walking up to his teacher and asking for a new textbook without being able to say the word is embarrassing to him. He fears his classmates will laugh at him. So, he does not say anything to his teacher. As a result, he isn't able to do his homework and gets a poor grade on the assignment that they had been given. If textbooks had been labeled in class, however, this student wouldn't have had this issue. He could have walked up to his teacher and explained the situation. This way he could have been given a new textbook or would have been allowed to photocopy the relevant pages of someone's textbook so that he could do his homework.

Even with all of this, students may sometimes face language barriers in class. This is why knowing which teachers on the school staff speak those students' language and therefore can help out in these cases is important. When students encounter such learning barriers and a teacher is unable to help them overcome them personally, she can turn to her colleagues, who are able to speak that student's language, for help.

However, being able to do so requires knowing which teachers and staff members are able to speak which languages. Teachers who want to have access to this kind of knowledge must conduct language inventories among the school staff. After all, they can't get to know every staff member and instructor personally, especially since some schools have hundreds of staff members on board.

Teachers can do school-wide language surveys to see who speaks which language. They can also gauge how proficient staff members are in the languages that they speak. Teachers must include staff members from the custodial department and food personnel in their surveys. You never know who can speak which language and will therefore be able to help you out in a moment of need. Not unless you ask. Conducting language surveys isn't just great for helping students overcome language barriers. It's also great for helping their parents and guardians if they're dealing with similar communication issues. Different staff members can be called into parent-teacher conferences and PTA meetings, for instance, and act as interpreters, making parent-teacher communication so much easier.

A key rule that teachers must keep in mind is that they shouldn't always wait for students to ask for help. Some students might be hesitant to confess that they don't understand a particular word, saying, or concept. They might worry about wasting their classmates' time, looking dumb, and being laughed at. As such, they might forgo asking questions. This will negatively impact them, as it'll prevent them from learning what they need to learn. To overcome this issue, teachers must check in regularly and frequently with their students. They must chat with them one-on-one, as opposed to before the entire class, to see how they're feeling about what they're learning. They must ask them if there's anything that they haven't understood fully. They must inquire whether their students have any questions for them. Of course, they must ask all these questions kindly and non-judgmentally. Otherwise, the very attitude they display to students will prevent them from explaining what they're having difficulty with and getting the help they need.

Finally, there is an array of learning traditional tools—such as books—and surveys, and worksheets teachers can use in class. The kinds of conventional tools that teachers use in class are essential as they play a part in whether or not students can see themselves in the subjects they're learning. The kinds of worksheets and surveys teachers use in class, particularly at the beginning of the year, can help them to get to know their students better. They can help them to learn more about their students' cultures and interests and thus become able to incorporate them into class. Considering all this, let's quickly go over what traditional learning tools and worksheets, and surveys can be used to this end:

- Books

    The kinds of books that are read in class and even just placed in classrooms can be essential. The students who read them and see them (or rather their covers) must be able to see themselves represented in those books. That doesn't mean that every single book should portray a character or family of a specific background. But it does mean that the books that are used in class must showcase a diverse cast of characters and families. Some examples of such books might be *My Name Is Sangoel* by Khadra Mohammed and Karen Lynn Williams, *The Invisible Man* by Ralph Ellison, and *Fry Bread* by Kevin Noble Maillard and Juana Martinez Neal. Remember: the more variety you have in the books you offer to your students, the more inclusive and therefore welcoming an environment you'll create.

- Student Interest Lists

  Ask your students what their specific interests are. Ask them about their cultures, cultural beliefs, and customs as well. Giving students assignments where they discuss such things can be a great way of finding all this out at the start of the school year or semester. Once you've discovered all this, prepare students' interest lists. Try to choose books that fit those interests. If a particular student is really interested in soccer, for instance, could you choose a book with a soccer star as its main character? Once you've made your choices and aligned them with your student's interests, you can take things a step further and have students read aloud from those books in class from time to time. Alternatively, you can have those students make presentations in class about the books you chose and participate in class discussions.

- Simple Questionnaires

  Getting to know each student can be a bit of a process, especially if you have over 20 students. Given that, you can make things easier for yourself by handing out student questionnaires. These work well at the start of the year when you don't really know much about your students. The questionnaires can be made up of all sorts of questions. For instance, they can ask students to share something special about their families. They can ask what languages the students speak and where they're from. Similarly, they can inquire if students have any specific habits or needs that their teacher should be aware of. If someone has ADHD and therefore constantly fidgets, for instance, that might be good to know.

- "All About Me" Questionnaire

  Another kind of questionnaire teachers can use is called the "All About Me" questionnaire. This is something that asks students all sorts of interest-focused questions like what makes them special and what their favorite movies, colors, and books are. It also asks students what they like most about their teachers and what they would change about their schools if they could. In asking these kinds of questions, teachers gain insight into how their students think and learn and what their preferences are.

- Short, Fun Drawings

  Sometimes questionnaires aren't enough. Sometimes teachers need just a little bit more to go on to get to know their students properly. This is where drawings can come in handy. Having students draw pictures of their favorite things like their favorite family celebration or favorite sports activity can allow teachers to get to know them quickly and easily. Having students draw pictures of how they like to celebrate accomplishments or the things that they want their teachers to know can do the same thing. All these activities can serve as windows into students' minds and hearts. Teachers can then use these windows to tailor their lessons and classes specifically for their students.

- Short, Fun Essays

  Having students write short (at max a page-long) essays can accomplish the same thing as the drawings. Except, of course, the essays will typically be more detailed than the drawings, giving teachers more information to go on. As part of such writing assignments, teachers can have students write about their families and favorite things to do for the things that make them special. They can even have students pair these short essays with drawings, thus making them more fun and multidimensional.

- The "Our Differences" Bulletin Board

Once you've gathered all these materials and gained valuable insights from them, you can use them to craft a special bulletin board. You can hang this board in class with the words, "Our Differences Make Us Special" written at the very top of it, in big, bold letters. You can choose one or two of each student's works and hang them on the bulletin board. If you decide to create such a board, try to choose works that truly showcase students' differences and the diversity that's to be found in class. In doing so, you can make them all feel represented.

Conclusion

It should be no surprise to anyone that traditional education and traditional teaching methods have been failing for some time. This is because the very widely accepted traditional education methods no longer fit the needs of the economic system we have established. Because while the values of our economic systems and job markets have changed, the values of the education system originally designed to cater to them have not. As such, it fails to answer students' needs, just as it fails to prepare them properly for the future ahead. Many students flounder at school as a result. Some students struggle academically and balk under the pressure that they are under. Unable to raise their grades in a system that neither takes their individuality nor their needs into account, many students drop out. Those that do stay aren't able to do well academically as they could have and this impacts both their future academic lives—such as which college they will go—and their future occupation and earnings severely. Put very simply, the traditional education system fails the students it was created for and fails societies as a whole as well. How could it not?

The way to solve this conundrum is actually fairly simple. Traditional education methods which no longer work—if they ever worked at all—must be dropped by the education system as a whole, in favor of methodologies that work. This is where culturally responsive teaching comes in. As we have seen throughout the majority of *The Promotion of Culturally Responsive Teaching,* this methodology takes different students' needs and individuality into account. It is a pedagogy that recognizes students' unique cultures, backgrounds, customs, experiences, and points of view, then uses them as educational tools. In other words, culturally responsive teaching takes all of these things that are familiar to students and makes them a part of the class. In doing so, it enables students to see themselves, their cultures, and their communities in both the classes they are in and the subject matter they are studying.

Culturally responsive teaching has countless benefits for students. For one, it motivates students and engages them in class because it makes their lessons more impactful, personal, and meaningful for them. For another, it helps students develop their critical thinking and problem-solving skills, which will be vital skills to have in the job market they will be entering in the future. Culturally responsive teaching also allows different students to understand each other's cultures and perspectives, thus creating an environment of tolerance and acceptance in class. This makes for a trusting environment and safe space, where students can form firm, trusting bonds with one another, as well as with their teacher. This increases their sense of belonging in class and bolsters their sense of self-esteem without causing them to disconnect from their cultural, ethnic, or racial identities. If anything, culturally responsive teaching strengthens these identities further.

The effect of all this is simple: culturally responsive teaching makes students more interested and engaged in their classes and academic lives. Simultaneously, it makes their parents and guardians and families more involved in their children's school lives. As a result, students' academic grades improve and their social bonds at school become stronger. All the while, the likelihood of their dropping out of school decreases. Students thus become more likely to keep pursuing their education beyond high school. This betters their chance of getting a good job and earning a decent salary. Put simply, culturally responsive teaching gives all students the same kinds of opportunities and access in both their schools and beyond, which is no less than any of them deserve. This is why culturally responsive teaching is so vital and should be adopted by all teachers and schools.

At the same time, culturally responsive teaching benefits parents and guardians. Parent participation in school is essential for students' academic success, as you've seen. Parent participation extends teaching outside of the classroom and school grounds. It enables parents to understand what their children are learning and dealing with at school. Thus, it equips them with the knowledge they need to help their children, be it with their homework or other issues. When parents become involved in their children's school and academic life, children perform better in school. Culturally responsive teaching methods permit and even encourage parents to participate more in school and school-related activities. By treating parents with the respect and understanding they deserve, culturally responsive teaching recruits them as teachers' partners in students' education. It establishes a sense of trust between parents and teachers, which increases communication between them. Thus, the two parties become more able to support students and meet students' needs. In short, culturally responsive teaching makes parents a greater part of their children's educational lives, thus increasing student success. This is one of the methodology's main benefits for parents and guardians, seeing as what they primarily want is to be there for their children and ensure they lead successful lives as strong, independent adults in the future.

Having a strong sense of identity is part and parcel of being a strong, independent adult leading a successful life. Students start building their sense of identity at a very young age. Their cultural identity is undoubtedly a part of their own, unique identity. Because of this, whether their unique cultures, value systems, and beliefs are welcomed and accepted on school grounds can impact their sense of identity. Culturally responsive teaching methods recognize this. The methodology supports and strengthens students' sense of identity by accepting their unique cultures and infusing them into classes and lessons. It infuses students with a sense of belonging when they're in class or at school. This empowers them and makes them feel respected and valued. It is on these feelings, these grounds that students start building their identity and their future successful lives.

Throughout this book, you have explored why culturally responsive teaching is so important and necessary for educators, students, and even parents and guardians. How can we, as the human race, expect to achieve any progress, after all, without accepting our many differences while denying the cultural commonalities between us? The simple answer is that we cannot. As you've seen, time and again, culturally responsive teaching methods can create the level, equal, equitable, and diverse playing fields that we, as a society and as individual human beings, need schools to be. You have also seen the value in this from multiple perspectives. You have read example after example of the power that lies in learning about other cultures. Learning about other cultures provides you, as a person and an educator, with an opportunity to create environments of mutual respect, understanding, equality, and inclusiveness. It gives you the ability to create said environment in your own classroom, populated by a generation of young minds that are the future of the world in every sense of the word.

Having seen all of this, you now have all the information you need to adopt and implement culturally responsive teaching methods. You can create the kind of safe learning environment you want for all of your students. You possess all the tools you need to truly understand, help, and support your students. So, go out there and use them to make a true difference!

If you've enjoyed this book and found it helpful, please leave a positive review!

Glossary

Absenteeism: a student regularly staying away from or avoiding work without having a valid excuse or reason.

Abuse: to treat someone with cruelty or violence regularly.

Accessibility: the quality of being reached, obtained, and used easily.

Aggression: feelings of anger or hostility that result in violent behavior.

Attention Deficit and Hyperactivity Disorder (ADHD): a neurodevelopmental disorder where the individual has difficulty focusing and controlling impulsive behaviors and is overly active.

Anxiety: a feeling of dread, fear, or uneasiness.

Assimilate: become similar.

Auditory learner: someone who learns best by hearing and listening.

Autism Spectrum Disorder (ASD): a developmental disability where the individual typically has difficulty in social interactions and engages in repetitive interests or behaviors.

Barrier to learning: anything that prevents learners from becoming fully engaged with the learning process.

Behavioral issue: a pattern of disruptive behaviors that last for more than 6 months.

Bias: prejudice for or against a person or a group of people.

Bilingual: being able to speak two languages fluently.

Bilingual education: education in an English-language school where children who aren't fluent in the language are taught in English and their native language.

Bullying: regular mistreatment or abuse of someone vulnerable by someone stronger.

Civil society: a society composed of citizens connected by common interests and collective activities.

Cognitive Behavior Therapy (CBT): a psychological treatment that is most often used to treat depression and anxiety disorders by changing thought patterns.

Cognitive growth: the development of how children think, explore things, and figure things out.

Cognitive skills: brain-based skills, which are needed to obtain knowledge and manipulate information and reason.

Communication skills: the ability to effectively share feelings and ideas with others.

Community: a group of people that live in the same place or share particular characteristics or beliefs

Cooperative base group: unchanging groups where group members' main goal is to help, support, and encourage one another.

Critical thinking skills: the ability to objectively analyze or evaluate a problem to arrive at a solution.

Culture: the beliefs, ideas, and costumes of a specific group of people or society.

Cultural barrier: situations grounded in cultural factors that can prevent the workings of educational systems.

Cultural belief: ideas common to the different individuals that make up a cultural group.

Cultural gap: a systemic difference between two cultures that hinders mutual understanding being reached.

Culturally responsive teaching: a pedagogy that uses students' own experiences, perspectives, characteristics, beliefs, customs, and values as educational tools within the classroom.

Curriculum: the subjects that make up a course of study in school.

Depression: feelings of despondency or severe dejection.

Digital divide: a gulf between those who have access to resources such as the internet, steady electricity, and computers and those that do not.

Disability: a mental or physical condition that limits a person's activities, movement, or senses.

Discipline: rules applied in school to manage student behaviors and the practices that are adopted to discourage unwanted behaviors.

Diversity: the practice of including people from a wide range of ethnic and social backgrounds, as well as of different sexual orientations and genders.

Dropout: a person who abandoned their education before graduation.

Education: the process of receiving systematic instruction at a place of learning such as a school or university.

Educator: The individual responsible for delivering education to students.

Equality: the idea that every student should have the same access to the same quality of education regardless of their background.

Equity: the process of taking the opportunities provided to students and enhancing them with the resources needed to turn the education field into a level playing field.

Emotional growth: a gradual increase in a person's capacity to experience, express, and interpret their full range of emotions and cope with them in a healthy way.

Empathy: being able to understand how other people feel or put yourself in their shoes.

Ethnicity: belonging to a social group that shares common cultural traditions or beliefs.

Gamifying: applying the elements of play into an educational process or activity.

Guardian: a person who has parental responsibility over a child without being their parent.

Guidance counselor: a person working at a school, advising students about their personal problems and career paths.

Homework: the schoolwork that students are required to do at home.

Implicit Association Test (IAT): a test that measures the associations between different concepts, evaluations, and stereotypes.

Implicit bias: having attitudes towards certain groups of people and associating them with certain stereotypes subconsciously.

Inclusion: the policy or practice of providing everyone with equal access to resources and opportunities regardless of their background.

Intercultural Communication Framework (ICT): the framework in which verbal and nonverbal interaction takes place between people of different cultural backgrounds.

Language barrier: a communication barrier between people who do not speak a common language.

Language gap: a lack of access to a specific language based on socio-economic factors.

Learning style: the way that different students learn.

Lecture: an educational talk to an audience.

Mental health: an individual's mental, emotional, and social well-being.

Methodology: a system of methods used in a particular field or area of study.

Multicultural: made up of a variety of different cultures.

Native speaker: a person who speaks a specific language from birth.

Non-native speaker: a person who is learning a language that is not their native one.

Non-traditional education: a kind of education that is offered to learners in ways that are different from those in traditional education.

Neglect: being uncared for and not being looked after.

Open source: a kind of software whose source code is made freely available to all and can be modified and/or redistributed.

Parent: a person's father or mother.

Parent participation: parents and guardians' involvement in their children's school and educational lives.

Parent Teacher Association (PTA): a local organization of parents and teachers that come together to promote close relations and improve the educational resources and facilities of schools.

Parent-Teacher Conference: a meeting between parents and teachers where the progress and learning of those parents' children are discussed.

Pedagogy: a method and practice of teaching.

Peer pressure: the influence the members of a group have on a person.

Positive reinforcement: the introduction of a desirable or pleasant stimulus after the desired behavior is exhibited.

Poverty: being extremely poor and lacking in resources.

Problem-solving skills: the ability to identify problems, brainstorm, analyze said problems, and come up with innovative solutions.

Retention: the measure of proportion of students who continue their education after the first year.

Safe space: a place in which a person can feel confident that they won't experience discrimination, harassment, criticism, or either physical or emotional harm.

Social skills: a person's ability to facilitate communication and interaction with others.

Social-emotional learning: a method of learning that aims to develop students' social and emotional skills.

Socio-economic barrier: social pressures and obstacles that prevent people from moving into more affluent positions.

Socio-economic status (SES): the social standing of an individual or a group of people.

Spatial skills: a person's ability to generate, retain and transform well-structured visual images.

Speech pattern: a distinctive manner of oral expression.

Stereotype: a fixed and oversimplified image or idea of a type of person or thing.

Stress: a state of emotional or mental tension that occurs when the individual is experiencing a great deal of pressure.

Student: a person who is studying at an educational institution.

Syllabus: the subjects in a course of study.

Talk therapy: treatment of mental, emotional, or behavioral issues through discussion, listening, and counseling.

Tradition: customs or beliefs that are handed down from generation to generation

Traditional education: the conventional and customary education system in place.

Trauma: a deeply disturbing or distressing experience.

Unemployment rate: the share of workers in the workforce that do not currently have a job but are actively looking for employment.

Visual learner: someone who learns best by reading or seeing pictures.

References

American Psychological Association. (2017, July). *Education and socioeconomic status.* American Psychological Association. https://www.apa.org/pi/ses/resources/publications/education

Baylor University. (2020, June 19). *6 ways educators can overcome language barriers with parents.* Baylor University. https://onlinegrad.baylor.edu/resources/language-barriers-parent-teacher-communication/

Burnham, K. (2020, July 31). *Culturally responsive teaching: 5 strategies for educators.* Northeastern University Graduate Programs. https://www.northeastern.edu/graduate/blog/culturally-responsive-teaching-strategies/

Caffarrella, R. S. (2010). *Viewing cultural barriers as opportunities to enhance learning: viewing cultural barriers as opportunities to enhance learning: an international perspective.* 2010 Conference Proceedings. Adult Education Research Conference, Sacramento, CA.

Casel. (2022). *What does the research say?* CASEL. https://casel.org/fundamentals-of-sel/what-does-the-research-say/

Centers for Disease Control. (2021, August 18). *Parent engagement in schools | adolescent and school health.* CDC. https://www.cdc.gov/healthyyouth/protective/parent_engagement.htm#:~:text=Research%20 shows%20that%20parent%20engagement

Christina, E. D. (2021). Dear Parents...Lessons from Your Child's Teacher. Warren Publishing, Incorporated.

Classtime Blog. (2017, July 7). *Challenging teacher biases to make your class stronger.* Classtime. https://www.classtime.com/blog/challenging-teacher-biases-to-make-your-class-stronger/

ColumbiaLearn. (2021). *What does inclusive teaching mean to you?* On YouTube. https://www.youtube.com/watch?v=-akUss3uj0M

Cowling, T. K. (2017, October 10). *Exploring cultures in your classroom: fun activities to try.* Hey, Teach! https://www.wgu.edu/heyteach/article/Exploring-Cultures-in-Your-Classroom-Activities-to-Try1710.html

de la Rosa, S. (2019, September 17). *Apps that connect teachers and parents can help overcome language barriers.* K-12 Dive. https://www.k12dive.com/news/apps-that-

connect-teachers-and-parents-can-help-
overcome-language-barriers/562958/

Decapua, A., & Wintergerst, A. C. (2016). Crossing
cultures in the language classroom. University
Of Michigan Press.

DeLuca, C., & Lam, C. Y. (2014). Preparing Teachers
for Assessment within Diverse Classrooms: An
Analysis   of   Teacher   Candidates'
Conceptualizations. *Teacher Education Quarterly*,
41(3),   3–24.
https://www.jstor.org/stable/teaceducquar.41.
3.3?read-
now=1&refreqid=excelsior%3A456c70cf15655
6c3612a43b9be72eb02&seq=13#page_scan_ta
b_contents

Destin, M., Hanselman, P., Buontempo, J., Tipton, E.,
& Yeager, D. S. (2019). Do Student Mindsets
Differ by Socioeconomic Status and Explain
Disparities in Academic Achievement in the
United   States?   *AERA   Open*,   5(3),
233285841985770.
https://doi.org/10.1177/2332858419857706

Dusek, J. B. (1975). Do teachers Bias Children's
Learning? *Review of Educational Research*, 45(4),
661–684. https://doi.org/10.2307/1170069

Egalite, A. J., Kisida, B., & Winters, M. A. (2015).
Representation in the classroom: The effect of
own-race teachers on student achievement.
Economics of Education Review, 45, 44–52.

https://doi.org/10.1016/j.econedurev.2015.01. 007

Faber, N. (2017, March 9). *Breaking through bias with parent/teacher home visits.* Medium; AFT. https://aftvoices.org/breaking-through-bias-with-parent-teacher-home-visits-a46142f27c1

Flygare, J., Hoegh, J. K., & Heflebower, T. (2021). Planning and Teaching in the Standards-Based Classroom. Marzano Resource.

Frederick, R., Donnor, J. K., & Hatley, L. (2009). Culturally Responsive Applications of Computer Technologies in Education: Examples of Best Practice. *Educational Technology*, 49(6), 9–13. https://www.jstor.org/stable/44429734?read-now=1&seq=4#page_scan_tab_contents

Gay, G. (2002). Preparing for Culturally Responsive Teaching. Journal of Teacher Education, 53(2), 106–116. https://doi.org/10.1177/0022487102053002003

Gay, G. (2010). Culturally responsive teaching: theory, research, and practice. Teachers College Press, Cop.

Geek & Sundry. (2018, March 13). *How "Assassin's Creed" is helping students learn about history.* Nerdist. https://nerdist.com/article/how-assassins-creed-is-helping-students-learn-about-history/

Generation T. (2021, November 4). *Why we need shop class back in schools more than ever.* We Are Generation T. https://www.wearegenerationt.com/buzz/articl e/why-we-need-shop-class-back-schools-more-ever?

Guido, M. (2017, September 14). *15 culturally-responsive teaching strategies and examples + downloadable list.* Prodigy Game. https://www.prodigygame.com/in-en/blog/culturally-responsive-teaching/

Hollie, S., & Allen, B. (2018). Culturally and Linguistically Responsive Teaching and Learning responsive teaching and learning; classroom practices for student success (2nd ed.). Huntington Beach Shell Education.

Howard, D. T. C. (2020, November 19). Culturally responsive teaching: 7 strategies and instruction Practices. HMHCO. https://www.hmhco.com/blog/culturally-responsive-teaching-strategies-instruction-practices#

Howard, G. R. (2016). *We can't teach what we don't know: white teachers, multiracial schools.* Teachers College Press.

Institute of Education Sciences. (2021). *What is culturally responsive teaching… and why does it matter?* On YouTube. https://www.youtube.com/watch?v=YCR_wp 1OOrY

Johnson, L. (2007). Rethinking successful school leadership in challenging U.S. schools: Culturally responsive practices in school-community relationships. *International Studies in Educational Administration*, 35.

Kentucky Department of Education. (2019). *Culturally responsive instruction*. Kentucky Department of Education. https://education.ky.gov/educational/diff/Pages/CulturallyResponsiveInstruction.aspx

Klepfer, J. (n.d.). *A desirable parental role*. California State University Bakersfield. https://www.csub.edu/~lwildman/finishedwebsite/parent.htm

Learning Portal. (n.d.). *Socioeconomic inequalities and learning*. Unesco IIEP Learning Portal. https://learningportal.iiep.unesco.org/en/issue-briefs/improve-learning/socioeconomic-inequalities-and-learning

Learning Sciences International. (2017, August 29). *When a new student has language barriers: 7 tips for teachers*. Learning Sciences International. https://www.learningsciences.com/blog/new-ell-students/

Mendler, A. N. (2021). Motivating Students Who Don't Care: Proven Strategies to Engage All Learners. Solution Tree Press.

Minasian, K. (2018). *20 ways to implement social emotional learning in your classroom: easy-to-follow steps to boost class morale & academic achievement.* S.T.O.R.M. Program.

Morrison, A. (2019, April 3). *Eight reasons why the traditional education system is broken.* Zarantech Training. https://www.zarantech.com/blog/eight-reasons-why-the-traditional-education-system-is-broken/

Mungia, K. (2017). Information Resource Addressing the Language Barrier: English Language Learners, Bilingual Education, and Learning Supports*. In Addressing the Language Barrier: English Language Learners, Bilingual Education, and Learning Supports*. http://smhp.psych.ucla.edu/pdfdocs/biling.pdf

National Association of Multicultural Education. (2014). *How do I know if my biases affect my teaching?* - NAME. https://www.nameorg.org/learn/how_do_i_know_if_my_biases_aff.php

National Center for Education Statistics. (2020). *COE - status dropout rate*s. National Center for Education Statistics.Nces.ed.gov. https://nces.ed.gov/programs/coe/indicator/coj/status-dropout-rates#:~:text=The%20overall%20status%20dropout%20rate

Network Support. (2019). *Helping students overcome language barriers in the classroom.* K12 Teacher Staff Development.

https://k12teacherstaffdevelopment.com/tlb/helping-students-overcome-language-barriers-in-the-classroom/

Orane, J. J. (2022). Teaching Methods That Work: 7 Culturally Responsive Strategies For Engaging Students and Raising Grades (p. 160). Independently Published.

PBS. (2019). *The role of parents.* PBS KIDS for Parents. https://www.pbs.org/parents/thrive/the-role-of-parents

Richard, G. T. (2017). Video Games, Gender, Diversity, and Learning as Cultural Practice: Implications for Equitable Learning and Computing Participation Through Games. *Educational Technology,* 57(2), 36–43. https://www.jstor.org/stable/44430522?read-now=1&seq=6#page_scan_tab_contents

Rodriguez, R. G., Lopez del Bosque, R., & Villareal, A. (2008, December). *Creating culturally responsive parent engagement – principal shares strategies for success.* IDRA. https://www.idra.org/resource-center/creating-culturally-responsive-parent-engagement/

Saluja, S. (2021, November 17). *6 Benefits of culturally responsive teaching.* SplashLearn. https://www.splashlearn.com/blog/why-culturally-responsive-teaching-is-important-for-students-growth/

Sandoval, J. (2020). *Introduction to Inclusive Teaching Practices.* On YouTube. https://www.youtube.com/watch?v=fpIsyKo-wKA

Sau Hou Chang. (2013). Instruction of Diverse Students in Mainstream Classrooms. Linus Books.

School of Education Blog. (2019, December 5). *Culturally Responsive Teaching: strategies and tips.* American University School of Education. https://soeonline.american.edu/blog/culturally-responsive-teaching

Snyder, S., & Diane Staehr Fenner. (2021). Culturally responsive teaching for multilingual learners: tools for equity. Corwin.

Truzy, T. (2017, August 6). 8 *Strategies to integrate culture in the classroom.* Owlcation. https://owlcation.com/academia/Cultural-Considerations-and-Strategies-for-the-Classroom

UNESCO. (2019, September 25). *Socio-cultural barriers to schooling.* Education | IIEP Policy Toolbox. International Institute for Educational Planning. https://policytoolbox.iiep.unesco.org/policy-option/socio-cultural-barriers-to-schooling/

University of Minnesota. (2016, April 8). 3.2 The Elements of Culture. Umn.edu; University of Minnesota Libraries Publishing edition, 2016. This edition adapted from a work originally produced in 2010 by a publisher who has requested that it not receive attribution. https://open.lib.umn.edu/sociology/chapter/3-2-the-elements-of-culture/

Vilorio, D. (2016, March 29). *Education matters: Career Outlook: U.S. Bureau of Labor Statistics.* US Bureau of Labor Statistics. https://www.bls.gov/careeroutlook/2016/data-on-display/education-matters.htm

Virginia Commonwealth University. (2015, February 13). *Why education matters to health: exploring the causes.* VCU. https://societyhealth.vcu.edu/work/the-projects/why-education-matters-to-health-exploring-the-causes.html

Weinstock, M. (2016, August 25). *Leonard Bernstein and the youngest, poorest symphony in the world.* New York City Center. https://www.nycitycenter.org/About/Blog/2016/leonard-bernstein-and-the-youngest-poorest-symphony-in-the-world/

Western Oregon University. (2010). *Anti-bias classroom observation checklist environmental evaluation.* http://5c2cabd466efc6790a0a-6728e7c952118b70f16620a9fc754159.r37.cf1.rackcdn.com/cms/AntiBiasChecklist-revised_2-2-15_1345.pdf

Image References

Clker Free Vector Images. *Circle Hands Teamwork.* [Illustration.] Pixabay. https://pixabay.com/vectors/circle-hands-teamwork-community-312343/

Gerd Altmann. *Students School Teacher.* [Illustration.] Pixabay. https://pixabay.com/vectors/students-school-teacher-knowledge-7282942/

Gordon Johnson. *Family people silhouette.* [Illustration.] Pixabay. https://pixabay.com/vectors/family-people-silhouette-child-dad-4989874/

Harish Sharma. *Kids Learn.* [Illustration.] Pixabay. https://pixabay.com/vectors/kids-learn-education-primary-1973917/

Maicon Fonseca Zanco. *Online Learning Call.* [Illustration.] Pixabay. https://pixabay.com/vectors/online-learning-call-webinar-5268393/

Mohamed Hassan. *Absorbed Book.* [Illustration.] Pixabay. https://pixabay.com/vectors/absorbed-book-girl-reading-student-2409314/

Mohamed Hassan. *Kids Study.* [Illustration.] Pixabay. https://pixabay.com/illustrations/kids-study-school-board-math-2439933/

Mohamed_Hassan. *Online Library Education Book.* [Illustration.] Pixabay. https://pixabay.com/illustrations/online-library-education-book-4091231/

Mohamed Hassan. *Principal Office*. [Illustration.] Pixabay. https://pixabay.com/vectors/principal-office-teacher-meeting-7141581/

Mohamed Hassan. *Science Lab Research*. [Illustration.] Pixabay. https://pixabay.com/vectors/science-lab-research-chemistry-6566158/

Mohamed Hassan. *Woman Education*. [Illustration.] Pixabay. https://pixabay.com/vectors/teacher-woman-education-chalkboard-6565166/

Moondance. *School Teacher Teaching Student*. [Illustration.] Pixabay. https://pixabay.com/illustrations/school-teacher-teaching-student-7103986/

Mote Oo Education *Myanmmar Teachers*. [Illustration.] Pixabay. https://pixabay.com/vectors/myanmar-burma-teachers-education-5204380/

Nugroho Dwi Hartawan. *Questions Man*. [Illustration.] Pixabay. https://pixabay.com/vectors/questions-man-head-success-lamp-2519654/

Open Clip Art Vectors. *Art Borders*. [Illustration.] Pixabay. https://pixabay.com/vectors/art-borders-boy-child-chromatic-2026073/

Pandannalmagen. *Education to Teach*. [Illustration.] Pixabay. https://pixabay.com/vectors/books-teacher-school-education-5171820/

Richard Duijnstee. *Teacher Student.* [Illustration.] Pixabay. https://pixabay.com/illustrations/teacher-student-school-education-2928817/

Rosy – The World Is Worth a Thousand Pictures. Teacher Students. [Illustration.] Pixabay. https://pixabay.com/illustrations/teacher-students-pupil-school-7531580/

Rosy – The World Is Worth a Thousand Pictures. *Teacher Students Pupil.* [Illustration.] Pixabay. https://pixabay.com/illustrations/teacher-students-pupil-school-7531578/

Sabine Da Silva. *Geometry Mathematics.* [Illustration.] Pixabay. https://pixabay.com/vectors/geometry-mathematics-protractor-1698595/

Made in the USA
Middletown, DE
16 September 2023

38624744R00088